How Much Is That In Real Money?

A Historical Commodity Price Index for Use as a Deflator of Money Values in the Economy of the United States

by

John J. McCusker

SECOND EDITION, REVISED AND ENLARGED

Worcester · American Antiquarian Society · 2001

Library of Congress Cataloging-in-Publication Data

McCusker, John J.
How much is that in real money? a historical commodity price index for use as a
deflator of money values in the economy of the United States / by John J. McCusker.
— 2nd ed., rev. and enlarged.
    p.   cm
Includes bibliographical references and index.
ISBN 1-929545-01-0 (pbk. : alk. paper)
    1. Prices—United States—History.   2. Consumer price indexes—United States—History.
3. Money—United States—History.   4. Value—History.   I. Title.

HB235.U6 M39 2001
332.4'973 21; aa05 02-06—dc01   2001022075

For Anna

Contents

Figures

Tables

Introduction

The applause of them that judge,
is the incouragement of those that write.
—John Dowland[1]

THIS IS A revised version of a monograph by the same title that was first published in the *Proceedings of the American Antiquarian Society*, 101 (October 1991): 297–373, and was then reprinted as a small book: *How Much Is That in Real Money?—A Historical Price Index for Use as a Deflator of Money Values in the Economy of the United States* (Worcester, Mass.: American Antiquarian Society, 1992). Corrections and additions to both were presented in the *Proceedings of the American Antiquarian Society*, 106 (October 1996): 315–22.

I wish to acknowledge with thanks the help of several people who have read and commented on my initial effort. Perhaps the single most noteworthy—and most appreciated—reaction to it was the column written by Dr. Martin E. Marty, the Fairfax M. Cone Distinguished Service Professor Emeritus of the History of Christianity, at The Divinity School, University of Chicago, in which he announced that 'the McCusker article turned me into a happy fool at the calculator.'[2] Using the commodity price index, he demonstrated all too conclusively that contributions to the Sunday collection plate aren't what they used to be. Marty's enthusiastic response to my initial publication—and similar communications from others—is a major cause of my own continuing enthusiasm for this topic, and the incentive for producing this

1. Dowland, *The Third and Last Booke of Songs or Ayres* (London: Thomas Adams, 1603), 'The Epistle to the Reader,' sig. A₂v.
2. Marty, 'Another 120 Days, Another $18.75,' *Christian Century*, 109, no. 25 (September 2, 1992): 791.

JOHN J. McCUSKER is the Ewing Halsell Distinguished Professor of American History and Professor of Economics at Trinity University in San Antonio, Texas.

new, revised, and expanded version. As John Dowland would have put it: 'My labours for my part I freely offer to everie mans judgement, presuming, that favour once attayned, is more easily encreased then lost.'

Besides routine stylistic changes, there are several more significant corrections and additions to this revised edition. As a matter of priority, the commodity price indexes for the United States and for Great Britain have been brought up to date. Of equal moment, the sources for obtaining the most recent index numbers have been altered to reflect the great advances in information technology over the last ten years. Readers are encouraged regularly to refresh the series in Tables A-1 and D-1 by adding the latest data themselves using these resources.

Attending to the past as well as the future, data have been added that move the United States commodity price index backward from 1700 to 1665 based on the recently published research of two very generous scholars, P. M. G. Harris and Stephen G. Hardy, who have shared their compilations and their insights with me. Thanks to them, I have also replaced the figures for the years 1700 through 1720 with clearly better data. The series for 1665–1720 has been calculated on a dollar basis, and the series from 1720 through 1770 has been recalculated, effectively putting it on a dollar basis also, and correcting an anomaly in the numbers originally presented. As requested by readers, I have provided more examples of the calculations for drawing the kinds of comparisons that this book is intended to facilitate. I have also added an appendix of exchange rate data that will allow for easier calculation of the differences between colonial values and post-1775 values. Surely of greatest importance, I reveal a solution to the question I posed about George Washington's teeth.

In addition to my gratitude for the moral support offered by Dr. Marty, I am also appreciative of the encouragement that John Hench and Caroline Sloat of the American Antiquarian Society have given me in the preparation of this second version of my thoughts on this subject. Many others have offered corrections and challenges; I am grateful to them all.[3] I did some of the work on the revisions to this volume while a 'scholar in residence' at the Rockefeller Study and Conference Center, Villa Serbelloni, Bellagio, Italy. I am very thankful to the Rockefeller Foundation and the good people at the Villa Serbelloni for their support and their kindness.

John J. McCusker
Trinity University
San Antonio, Texas

3. Among the comments offered was a review of the book by Winifred Rothenberg in *Business History Review*, 67 (Autumn 1993): 462–65, to which I replied (*ibid.*, 68 [Summer 1994]: 276–79). Employing the language of diplomacy, let me say that we had a frank exchange of views. The attention she paid to the first version has allowed me to clarify and sharpen this second edition, although perhaps not to the degree she may have wished. I am grateful for her suggestions.

In a case of simple serendipity, two Swedish writers and an English author seem to have been working on projects parallel to my own, all of us unbeknownst to the others. For the former, see Lars O. Lagerqvist and Ernst Nathorst-Böös, *Vad kostade det?: Priser och löner från medeltid til våra dagar*, [3d ed., rev.] (Stockholm: LTs Förlag, [1993]). The first edition of their work apparently appeared in 1984; the second edition in 1985. For the latter, see Lionel M. Munby, who published a pamphlet titled *How Much Is That Worth?* [1st ed.] ([Salisbury, England]: British Association for Local History, [1989]). He issued a second, revised edition of his pamphlet in 1996. In different but analogous ways, they do for their countries what this study does for the United States.

Among other works that parallel my own, three are worth mentioning in particular. Cutting a bit close to the bone is the article by James C. Cooper and Kark Borden, 'Public Representation of Historical Prices: An Interdisciplinary Opportunity,' *Essays in Economic and Business History: The Journal of the Economic and Business Historical Society*, 14 (1996): 465–85. It would be pleasant if borrowers of an idea at least acknowledged those from whom they borrowed. Elements of this book have also been used—in these instances with full attribution—on several websites. See, for instance, the sites maintained by Roy Davies of the University of Exeter ('Money—Past, Present & Future—Sources of Information on Monetary History, Comtemporary Developments, and the prospects for Electronic Money,' http://www.ex.ac.uk/-Rdavies/arian/money.html); and Ronald W. Michener ('The Leslie Brock Center for the Study of Colonial Currency,' http://www.virginia.edu/-econ/brock.html).

The EH.Net feature, 'How Much Is That?' (http://www.eh.net) uses the data in Table 1, Column 6, and Table D-1, Column 4, as the basis for some of its tables with the author's consent and full attribution. EH.Net operates the Economic History Services fileserver and several electronic discussion lists to provide resources and promote communication among scholars in economic history and related fields.

How Much Is That In Real Money?

Yes, sir. They were, as the expression goes, real money.
—Neal Stephenson[1]

B UT how much is that in **real** money?' It is a question that
lurks behind the mention of the price of anything in the
past, from the cost of George Washington's false teeth to
the worth of the gold doubloon that Herman Melville's Captain
Ahab nailed to his ship's mast as the reward to the first of his crew
to sight Moby Dick. Teachers of history mention wages or prices
at their peril, certain in the knowledge that someone will ask the
question and equally certain that they will have a hard time an-
swering it. Economic historians in departments of history are expected to be able to pronounce instantly on the modern value of
the Biblical shekel, of medieval Venetian money, and of World
War I reparations—for students and for colleagues, both. Economic historians in departments of economics have it easier because economists are supposed to be able to find out such things
for themselves, however difficult the exercise may turn out to be.
What follows is intended as a guide to all who would like to compare the changing value of things over time in real terms, at least
with regard to the United States economy.

Writers on economic matters have long recognized the need to
reduce prices to constant value terms if the comparisons they wish
to draw are to make any sense. They have not been equally unan-
imous in their choice of what to employ as the standard against
which to measure the value of other things. Indeed there have
been considerable differences of opinion as to what makes the
best basis for such comparisons. A continuing contender has been
the worth of an individual's labor. Economic theorists as disparate

1. Neal Stephenson, *Snow Crash* (New York: Bantam Books, [1992]), 104.

as Adam Smith, Benjamin Franklin, and Karl Marx have argued
for a labor theory of value. According to Smith:

> Labour . . . is the only universal, as well as the only accurate
> measure of value, or the only standard by which we can com-
> pare the values of different commodities at all times and at all
> places. We cannot estimate, it is allowed, the real value of dif-
> ferent commodities from century to century by the quantities
> of silver which were given for them. We cannot estimate it year
> by year by the quantities of corn. By the quantities of labour we
> can, with the greatest accuracy, estimate it both from century to
> century and from year to year.[2]

Just as Adam Smith suggested, the two alternatives to his labor
theory of value have been the value of precious metals, usually
gold and silver, and the value of commodities. While the last of
these, the value of commodities, has clearly won out as the accepted measure of changes in value over time, there are still those
who agree with Smith that wage rates are the best deflator,[3] while

2. Adam Smith, *An Inquiry into the Nature and Causes of the Wealth of Nations* (1776), ed.
R[oy] H. Campbell, A[ndrew] S. Skinner, and W[illiam] B. Todd, 2 vols. (Oxford: Clarendon Press, 1976), 1:54. Cf. 1:47, 51, 328–29. Despite what he stated in these passages,
Smith elsewhere (1:67) rejected the notion, so essential to Marx, that labor was the exclu-
sive determiner of prices in a capitalist economy. See Ronald L. Meek, *Smith, Marx, & After: Ten Essays in the Development of Economic Thought* (London: Chapman & Hall, 1977),
7–8. For an introduction to this subject and a bibliography, see Donald F. Gordon, 'Value,
Labor Theory of,' in *International Encyclopedia of the Social Sciences*, ed. David L. Sills, 17
vols. ([New York:] The Macmillan Company & The Free Press, [1968]), 16:279–83. See
also Terence [W.] Hutchison, *Before Adam Smith: The Emergence of Political Economy,
1662–1776* (Oxford: Basil Blackwell, [1988]), 364–65 passim.

For Franklin, see his *A Modest Inquiry into the Nature and Necessity of a Paper-Currency*
(Philadelphia: New Printing Office, 1729), 18–23; and as reprinted with commentary in
The Papers of Benjamin Franklin, ed. Leonard W. Labaree et al., in progress (New Haven:
Yale University Press, 1959 to date), 1:141–57. Note that, just as William A. Wetzel
pointed out in *Benjamin Franklin as an Economist* (Johns Hopkins University Studies in
Historical and Political Science, 13th Ser., No. 9 [Baltimore: Johns Hopkins University
Press, 1895], 18–22, 30–32), Franklin borrowed heavily in this matter from both the ideas
and the words of [William Petty], *A Treatise of Taxes & Contributions: Shewing the Nature and
Measures of Crown-Lands* . . . (London: N[athaniel] Brooke, 1662).

For Marx, see his *Capital: A Critique of Political Economy*, ed. Friedrich Engels, trans. and
ed. Samuel Moore and Edward [B.] Aveling, revised by Ernest Untermann, 3 vols.
(Chicago: Charles H. Kerr and Co., 1906–1909), 3:41–55 and passim. See also, Ronald L.
Meek, *Studies in the Labour Theory of Value* (2d ed.; London: Lawrence & Wishart, 1973).

3. For proponents of the value of labor as a long-term price deflator, see, e.g., Stanley
Lebergott, 'Wage Trends, 1800–1900,' in *Trends in the American Economy in the Nineteenth*

others prefer gold or silver.[4] Commodity prices have won out because an index based on them has the advantage of integrating the value of all the things that go into them, including the value of the work employed in their production. The cost of commodities embodies the value added by labor. The commodity price index has been and continues to be the preferred basis for comparing values over time.

One may, of course, create a price index number series out of the changing values of anything for which we have a series of prices. Some have called, facetiously, for a diamond price index, presumably justified by the maxim that 'diamonds are a girl's best friend.'[5] Others have argued, more seriously, for a labor price index, as we have just read. Each would measure, relative to a base period, the rise and fall in the value of diamonds or wages or

---

Century, ed. William N. Parker, National Bureau of Economic Research, Studies in Income and Wealth, Vol. 24 (Princeton, N.J.: Princeton University Press, 1960), 449–99; Lebergott, *Manpower in Economic Growth: The American Record since 1800* (New York: McGraw-Hill, 1964); the discussion in Alice Hanson Jones, *American Colonial Wealth: Documents and Methods*, 2d ed., 3 vols. (New York: Arno Press, 1978), 3:1728–29; and David S. Landes, *The Wealth and Poverty of Nations: Why Some Are So Rich and Some So Poor* (New York: W. W. Norton & Company, [1998]), 161, n. *.

4. For some concerns about the use of precious metals for this purpose, see Earl J. Hamilton, 'Use and Misuse of Price History,' in *The Tasks of Economic History: Papers Presented at the Fourth Annual Meeting of the Economic History Association—A Supplemental Issue of the Journal of Economic History*, [Supplement 4] (New York, 1944), 48; Hamilton, *War and Prices in Spain, 1651–1800*, Harvard Economic Studies, Vol. 81 (Cambridge: Harvard University Press, 1947), 232.

A critical obstacle to using precious metals or labor to construct long-term indexes is the lack of adequate data. Two recent books by Roy W. Jastram on the historical fluctuations in the value of precious metals illustrate this difficulty: *The Golden Constant: The English and American Experience, 1560–1976* (New York: John Wiley & Sons, [1977]); and *Silver: The Restless Metal* (New York: John Wiley & Sons, [1981]). The author encountered considerable problems finding data for the period prior to the beginning of the nineteenth century and relied instead on nominal mint values and other official government sources rather than market prices. Compare John J. McCusker, *Money and Exchange in Europe and America, 1600–1775: A Handbook* (2d ed.; Chapel Hill: University of North Carolina Press, [1992]), 13–17; and K[irti] N. Chaudhuri, *The Trading World of Asia and the English East India Company, 1660–1760* (Cambridge: Cambridge University Press, 1978), 162–63. The 'second edition' of *Money and Exchange in Europe and America* made reference to here was issued in 1992, although the publication information in the book failed to say so. There were many and some rather significant corrections in that reissue of the original version. I call attention to it only to alert the interested reader to check terms and data before using the earlier version.

5. As in the title of the song written by Jule Styne and Leo Robin for the 1949 musical comedy *Gentlemen Prefer Blondes* ([New York]: Columbia Records, [1950]).

whatever. To know that the cost of labor doubled over a given period in several different economies by comparing index numbers for wages in those economies could be useful. What would be unacceptable is the extension of any such single-item index number to an entire economy by using it to deflate the values of other things. To be told that the cost of television sets relative to wages, or diamonds, fell by 50 percent is almost useless.

By contrast, to discover that, relative to all commodities, the price of television sets fell by 50 percent says a great deal more. This statement tells us that among the choices available to consumers, this one item became significantly less costly when compared with all other goods. Indeed, since the commodity price index necessarily includes a labor component, if only because changes in the prices of goods are due in part to changes in the costs of producing them, then we have learned that, relative to the whole economy, the cost of television sets has shifted significantly. We are encouraged as a consequence to investigate why and how this was so. It follows that a price index based on commodities, reflecting the market basket of all goods and services, offers the better choice for establishing, relative to an entire economy, changes in the value of one part of it, such as wage rates. The fact is that the 'real value' of labor is best measured when its price is deflated using a commodity price index. To know how much a person's work can buy is to know the worth of labor in 'real money.'

A commodity price index is a statistical tool designed to accomplish comparisons of real money values over time by filtering out the impact of any differences in the value of money itself.[6] The ef-

---

6. There are several wide-ranging introductions to the subject of index numbers, among which the first two are considered masterworks. See Wesley C. Mitchell, 'The Making and Using of Index Numbers,' in *Index Numbers of Wholesale Prices in the United States and Foreign Countries*, United States, Department of Labor, Bureau of Labor Statistics, Bulletin No. 284 (Washington, D.C.: United States Government Printing Office, 1921), 7–114; and Irving Fisher, *The Making of Index Numbers: A Study of Their Varieties, Tests, and Reliability*, 3d ed., rev. (Boston: Houghton Mifflin Co., 1927). See also Walter R. Crowe, *Index Numbers: Theory and Application* (London: Macdonald & Evans Ltd., 1965); Bruce D. Mudgett, *Index Numbers* (New York: John Wiley & Sons, 1951); Jacqueline Fourastié, *Les for-*

fect of using a commodity price index to answer the question asked at the start of this exercise is analogous to what one does using foreign exchange rates to convert foreign currencies into one's own money in order to make more comprehensible the prices of goods and services in other places. Even the calculations entailed, simple division or multiplication, are much the same in both cases. The numbers produced, if only because they permit us a clearer view of the reality behind the original figures, are often referred to as the 'real' values.[7] More usually, in comparisons of prices or trade data, we talk of the original figures as having been stated in 'current' dollars (or pounds or yen) and the indexed prices as being stated in 'constant' dollars (or pounds or yen).[8]

A commodity price index is only one kind of index number. Index numbers, which effectively reduce data series to percentages, may be calculated for any serial data, not just for prices. An index number 'measures the magnitude of a variable relative to a specified value,' called the reference base.[9] We resort to the index in order to enhance our perception of changes in a series by expressing the data as a percentage of a reference base. The index number is the systematic expression of the percentage increases or decreases that any number in the series represents when com-

---

mules d'indices de prix: Calculs numériques et commentaires théoriques (Paris: Librairie Armand Colin, 1966); R[onald] F. Fowler, *Some Problems of Index Number Construction*, Studies in Official Statistics, Research Series, No. 3 (London: Her Majesty's Stationery Office, 1970); [F. A. Fitzpatrick], *Wholesale Price Index: Principles and Procedures*, Studies in Official Statistics, No. 32 (London: Her Majesty's Stationery Office, [1980]); and Ralph Turvey, *Consumer Price Indexes: An ILO Manual* (Geneva, Switzerland: International Labour Office, 1989). For a useful overview of the subject, see Erik Ruist, Ethel D. Hoover, and Philip J. McCarthy, 'Index Numbers,' *International Encyclopedia of the Social Sciences*, ed. Sills, 7:154–69. These essays include valuable bibliographies.

7. At least one hapless historian confused 'real' with 'actual' (as opposed to nominal) and wrongly labeled a current value series of export figures as the 'real' values. He wishes here to recant his error. See John J. McCusker, 'The Current Value of English Exports, 1672 to 1800,' *William and Mary Quarterly*, 3d Ser., 28 (October 1971): 607–28, as revised and emended in McCusker, *Essays in the Economic History of the Atlantic World* (London: Routledge, 1997), 222–44, where the mistake has been corrected.

8. On the appropriateness—even the necessity—of the use of 'real' prices or 'real' values for historical analyses, see Robert William Fogel, *Without Consent or Contract: The Rise and Fall of American Slavery* (New York: W. W. Norton & Company, 1989), 432, n. 7.

9. Ruist, 'Index Numbers: Theoretical Aspects,' *International Encyclopedia of the Social Sciences*, ed. Sills, 7:154.

pared against the reference base number (for instance: 'it increased 80 percent' or 'it fell to 20 percent of its former value').

Index numbers are especially useful for two purposes. They permit comparisons to be drawn among several parallel series more easily than we could from the disparate data. This is especially true when all of the index numbers are expressed in terms of reference base numbers dated to the same period. Index numbers are also useful because they transform the data in ways that allow for additional statistical analysis. Consequently they have been widely employed by economists, economic historians, and, in fact, by any researcher or analyst who deals with series of numbers.

Using commodity prices to construct index numbers of the value of things has an impressive pedigree. In the eighteenth century, several major European political economists employed commodity price indexes in their analyses: the Englishman Bishop William Fleetwood, the Frenchmen Charles Dutot and Nicolas François Dupré de Saint-Maur, and the Italian Count Gian Rinaldo Carli.[10] In the 1740s and again in the 1780s the Massachu-

10. [William] Fleetwood, *Chronicon Preciosum: or, An Account of English Gold and Silver Money, the Price of Corn, and Other Commodities, . . . &c. in England, for Six Hundred Years Last Past*, [rev. ed.] (London: T[homas] Osborne, 1745); [Charles de Ferrare Dutot], *Réflexions politiques sur les finances et le commerce. Où l'on examine quelles ont été sur les revenus, les denrées, le change étranger, & conséquemment sur notre commerce, les influences des augmentations et les diminutions des valeurs numéraires des monnoyes*, 2 vols. (The Hague: V[aillant] and N[icolas] Prevost, 1738); [Nicolas François Dupré de Saint-Maur], *Recherches sur la valeur des monnoies, et sur le prix des grains, avant et après le Concile de Francfort [1409]* (Paris: Nyon, Didot and Saugrain, 1762); and Giovanni Rinaldo Carli, *Delle Monete e dell'Instituzione delle Zecche d'Italia, dell'Antico, e Presente Sistema d'Esse e del Loro Intrinseco Valore, e Rapporto con la Presente Moneta dalla Decadenza dell'Impero sino Secolo XVII*, 3 pts. in 4 vols. (Mantua: n.p., 1754; Pisa: Giovan Paolo Giovannelli, e Compagni, 1757; and Lucca: Jacopo Giusti, 1760). For discussions of these works see Mitchell, 'Making and Using of Index Numbers,' in *Index Numbers of Wholesale Prices*, 7–10; Fisher, *Making of Index Numbers*, 458–60; and Crowe, *Index Numbers*, 97–99 ff. As an addition to Fleetwood, see *An Account of the True Market-Price of Wheat, and Malt, at Windsor, for 100 Years. Begun & Published by Wm. Fleetwood B[isho]p of Ely from 1646 to 1706. And Since Continued in the Same Manner* (London: n.p., 1745 [?]). For more about Fleetwood, who published his first edition in 1707, see G[eorge] N. Clark, 'The Occasion of Fleetwood's "Chronicon Preciosum",' *English Historical Review*, 60 (October 1936): 686–90. For more about Carli, whose third volume, *Del Valore, e della Proporzione de' Mettali Monetati con i Generi in Italia prima delle Scoperte dell'Indie; Col Confronto della Proporzione de' Tempi Nostri* is of particular interest, see Ch[arles] Coquelin and [Gilbert Urbain] Guillaumin, *Dictionnaire de l'économie politique*, 3rd ed., 2 vols. (Paris: Guillaumin & Cie., 1864), 1:289–90. The concerns of Fleetwood, Dutot, Dupré and Carli were shared by contemporaries at levels other than simply the theoretical. See, for instance, the seventeenth-century debate over the property requirement for jurors as sum-

setts General Court put theory into practice through legislation crafted to offset the loss in the value of money during two different periods of inflation by making payments more equitable. This was obviously an early form of indexing.[11] The impetus in the second instance was complaints about losses in the purchasing power of soldiers' pay caused by the depreciation in the worth of the state's currency during the American Revolutionary War.[12] Elsewhere over the past two centuries, episodes of sudden, sharp change in the purchasing power of money have similarly whetted interest in the therapeutic value of the commodity price index.[13]

The wider appreciation over time of the usefulness of commodity price indexes has resulted in a honing of the theory of index numbers, a broadening in their application, more research into the history of price behavior, and the computation of more and better historical price indexes.[14] Both economists and histo-

---

marized in James C. Oldham, 'The Origins of the Special Jury,' *University of Chicago Law Review*, 50 (Winter 1983): 144–50.

11. See Willard C. Fisher, 'The Tabular Standard in Massachusetts History,' *Quarterly Journal of Economics*, 27 (May 1913): 417–51. For the 1740s, see also *A Table Shewing the Value of Old Tenor Bills, in Lawful Money* ([Boston: Samuel Kneeland and Timothy Green (?), 1750]). For the 1780s, see also [Massachusetts (Colony), Laws and Statutes], *The Acts and Resolves, Public and Private, of the Province of the Massachusetts Bay*, [ed. Abner Cheney Goodell et al.], 21 vols. (Boston, Massachusetts: Wright and Porter, 1869–1922), 5:1133–37, 1277–95. For the compiled 'mean rate of depreciation,' 1777–80, see 5:1288. See also the *Scale of Depreciation, Agreeable to An Act of the (Now) Commonwealth of Massachusetts, Passed September 29, 1780* ([Boston: n.p., 1781]); and *Scale of Depreciation, Agreeable to An Act of the Commonwealth of Massachusetts, Passed September 29, 1780, to be Observed as a Rule for Settling the Rate of Depreciation on All Contracts, Public and Private, for the Payment of Monies Made on Or Since the First Day of January, 1777* ([Boston]: T. & J. Fleet, [1781]). At the end of the American Revolution other state governments in addition to Massachusetts passed similar laws and issued similar tables, for which see Appendix C, n. 9, below.

12. For more details of the American wartime experience with inflation and depreciation, see Appendix C, below.

13. See, e.g., the many guides that were published consequent to the depreciation of French currency in the 1790s, for example, P. V. N. Vigneti, *Changes faits sur le cours des papiers-monnoies, depuis leur origine, 31 août 1789, jusqu'au 30 ventôse de l'an IV . . . auquel on a joint un tableau progressif de dépréciation vraie . . .* (Paris: Gueffier and the Author, 1797). See also Eugene N. White, 'Measuring the French Revolution's Inflation: The Tableaux de dépréciation,' *Histoire & Mesure*, 6 (Nos. 3/4, 1991): 245–74. Compare the 'Aldrich Report' of 1893: [United States, Congress, Senate Committee on Finance], *Wholesale Prices, Wages, and Transportation: Report by Mr. [Nelson W.] Aldrich, from the Committee on Finance, March 3, 1893*, 52d Congress, 2d Session, Senate Report No. 1394 [Serial Set No. 3074 (4 pts.)] (Washington, D.C.: United States Government Printing Office, 1893).

14. Arthur H. Cole and Ruth Crandall, 'The International Scientific Committee on

rians have been active in these pursuits. Historians have employed the evolving theoretical constructs of the economist in their study of early economic behavior; economists have turned to the past in order to test and refine index number theory. Significant—not only as the occasion for the present discussion—is the progressively earlier application of all this research, for Great Britain

---

Price History,' *Journal of Economic History*, 24 (September 1964): 381–88, described much of the research into price history done during the 1930s as an outgrowth of the monetary disruptions in the United States and Europe during the decade of the Great Depression. See also *I Prezzi in Europa del XIII Secolo a Oggi*, ed. Ruggiero Romano ([Turin]: Guilio Einaudi, [1967]); and Gísli Gunnarsson, 'A Study in the Historiography of Prices,' *Economy and History*, 19 (1976): 124–41. This massive enterprise, only a part of which saw publication, provided the raw materials for most of the work that is the focus of this book. For the United States, see especially the summary of the price history for the years before the Civil War compiled by Arthur Harrison Cole, *Wholesale Commodity Prices in the United States, 1700–1861*, 2 vols. (Cambridge: Harvard University Press, 1938). See also the studies cited on p. 43, in Appendix A, n. 4. The most famous of the inquiries into European prices are William [Henry] Beveridge, *Prices and Wages in England from the Twelfth to the Nineteenth Century* (London: Longmans Green and Co., 1939); and N[icolaas] W. Posthumus, *Nederlandsche Prijsgeschiedenis*, 2 vols. (Leiden: E. J. Brill, 1943–1964).

There are important archival collections associated with all three of the Cole, Beveridge, and Posthumus studies, each containing a great deal of additional material: Records of the International Scientific Committee on Price History, 1928–39, Manuscript and Archives Division, Baker Library, Graduate School of Business Administration, Harvard University, Boston, Massachusetts; William Beveridge Papers, Wages and Prices Collection, Manuscript Department, British Library of Political and Economic Science, London School of Economics and Political Science; and the Collectie Commerciële Couranten, 15e–19e Eeuw, and the Collectie N. W. Posthumus, 1919–49, both in the Nederlandsch Economisch-Historisch Archief, at the Internationaal Instituut voor Sociale Geschiedenis, Amsterdam. For the Beveridge collection, see G. A. Falla, *A Catalogue of the Papers of William Henry Beveridge, 1st Baron Beveridge* ([London:] British Library of Political and Economic Science, 1981). For Posthumus's papers and the materials he collected, see Peter Boorsma and Jan Lucassen, *Gids van de Collecties van het Nederlandsch Economisch-Historisch Archief te Amsterdam*, Nederlandsch Economisch-Historisch Archief, Ser. 5, No. 6 (Amsterdam: Nederlandsch Economisch-Historisch Archief, 1992), 158–59, 176; and Boorsma and Joost van Genabeek, *Commercial and Financial Serial Publications of the Netherlands Economic History Archives: Commodity Price Currents, Foreign Exchange Rate Currents, Stock Exchange Rate Currents and Auction Lists, 1580–1870*, Nederlandsch Economisch-Historisch Archief, Inventarisatie Bijzondere Collecties 4 (Amsterdam: Nederlandsch Economisch-Historisch Archief, 1991). Additional materials are in the Frank Ashmore Pearson Papers, Albert R. Mann Library, Cornell University, Ithaca, N.Y.; and the '(Industrial Research Department), Wholesale Prices' Collection, Wharton School of Finance and Commerce, University of Pennsylvania, Philadelphia. When I consulted this last collection—essentially the papers of Dr. Anne Bezanson and her colleagues—in May 1971, it was in the care of Professor Dorothy S. Brady of the Department of Economics of the Wharton School. She died in 1977. My attempts in 1994 and 1995 to discover the current location of the collection proved fruitless despite the enthusiastic assistance of such people as Stephen Lehmann of the Van Pelt Library and Sue Torelli of the Center for Human Resources of the Wharton School, to both of whom I extend my thanks. I hope that these materials will someday be found—and that, when they are, someone will tell me.

back into the late medieval period, for the United States now to the last third of the seventeenth century.

The attention given to commodity price indexes has also provoked research into the best ways to compile all index numbers.[15] This is even truer of index numbers that combine several elements, particularly general price indexes. The computation of a price index for a single commodity is a comparatively easy matter and involves the reduction of each value to a simple percentage of the reference base value, a 'price relative.' The computation of a general price index raises the issue of how to account for the differing degrees of importance among the various commodities the prices of which are to be aggregated into the single index number, especially when the relative importance of commodities has shifted over time. For instance, if an index is composed of the prices of both diamonds and wheat, we have three choices: to assign each of them equal importance (or weight); to permit them to be 'self-weighted' proportionate simply to the differences in their money costs; or to impose some scheme for apportioning between them different weights based, perhaps, on some measure of their relative significance in an economy. The realization of the first and last of these choices requires statistical processing of the price data before the index is computed. The second option, 'self-weighting,' while making the index easier to calculate, risks possible erroneous results, such as a price index that might indicate a broad rise in prices when only the price of diamonds really rose.[16]

Compilers of modern price indexes, having the dual advantage of sufficient data and increasingly faster computers, are able to test very elaborate weighting schemes. By and large, researchers have found that the best commodity price indexes are ones care-

15. This and subsequent paragraphs merely summarize the universally accepted (and, therefore, the non-controversial) points from the standard studies. See text, n. 6, above, for the works by Mitchell, Fisher, and Crowe. Thus, there are no detailed citations for what follows—unless some work states a point in a manner that seems particularly cogent. Furthermore, the discussion in Mitchell, 'Making and Using of Index Numbers,' in *Index Numbers of Wholesale Prices*, can be recommended as particularly useful for the economic historian and the explanations in Crowe, *Index Numbers*, as especially easy to understand.

16. Fisher, *Making of Index Numbers*, 333, cites two classic examples of 'freakishness' caused by eccentric commodities. On this whole subject see also pp. 439–50.

fully weighted to reflect the relative importance of several different commodities in an economy. Nevertheless, indexes computed
in all three ways tend to move roughly in tandem, changing direction at about the same times and to about the same degree.
The key to the successful commodity price index rests in the
choice of commodities. It is essential that one be sensitive to the
'utility value' of such commodities. As a consequence, self-
weighted (or 'implicitly weighted') indexes that avoid eccentric
commodities tend to be almost as good as weighted series.

Such results are reassuring to the compilers and users of historical series, who rarely have enough data to construct weighted
indexes and who are usually forced by circumstances to adopt the
weighting implicit in the differences in the magnitude of the
prices themselves. Equally do we who work with historical series
take comfort in the realization that commodity prices in any
economy are interdependent upon one another, that the price of
flour, for instance, is a function not only of the price of wheat, but
also of the cost of the labor to produce it and the machines to
grind it (labor costs and machine costs being themselves in-
fluenced by the prices of such things as flour and bread).

An index based on a few selected commodities can do almost as
good a job of tracing the prevailing level of prices as can a
weighted price index compiled from the prices of many different
commodities. Thus one of the most important modern practi-
tioners of the art, Earl J. Hamilton, once observed: 'Price historians have not infrequently discovered, to their dismay, . . . that previously compiled index numbers based on the quotations of a very
few articles—sometimes two or three—haphazardly thrown to-
gether from heterogeneous sources for widely scattered years
have disclosed the trend of prices almost as accurately as their la-
boriously constructed indices from homogeneous series embrac-
ing monthly or quarterly quotations for dozens of commodities.'[17] The reason, according to Wesley C. Mitchell, perhaps the

17. Hamilton, 'Use and Misuse of Price History,' 50. Compare Hamilton, *War and Prices in Spain*, 112–13.

most important theoretician on the subject, is that 'the price changes of practically every commodity in the markets of the whole country are causally related to the changes in the prices of a few or of many, perhaps in the last resort of all, other commodities that are bought and sold.'[18]

Another issue in the compilation of price indexes has to do with the mathematics of the actual computation. First, as suggested above, the question to be asked is: does one use the prices themselves directly, totaled and divided by the reference base number — the aggregate or 'market basket' method; or does one first com-

---

18. Mitchell, 'Making and Using of Index Numbers,' in *Index Numbers of Wholesale Prices*, 39. Compare Fisher, *Making of Index Numbers*, 331–40. Concerning Mitchell, see *Wesley Clair Mitchell: The Economic Scientist*, ed. Arthur F. Burns (New York: National Bureau of Economic Research, 1952).

It is absolutely necessary to reiterate the verdict of experts on this point because some writers, perhaps unaware of the literature on index numbers and the compilation of price indexes, seem willing to deny the usefulness of historical commodity price indexes based simply on a contention—irrelevant though it may be—that a given index was compiled using too few commodities. See, e.g., Ralph Davis, *The Industrial Revolution and British Overseas Trade* (Leicester, England: Leicester University Press, 1979), 79; Leslie V. Brock, *The Currency of the American Colonies, 1700–1764: A Study in Colonial Finance and Imperial Relations* ([Ph.D. diss., University of Michigan, 1941]; New York: Arno Press, 1975), 'Preface'; Julian Gwyn, 'British Government Spending and the North American Colonies, 1740–1775,' *Journal of Imperial and Commonwealth History*, 8 (January 1980): 84, n. 12; and Peter H. Lindert, 'Probates, Prices, and Preindustrial Living Standards,' in *Inventaires après-décès et ventes de meubles: Rapports à une histoire de la vie économique et quotidienne (XIVe–XIXe siècles)*, ed. Micheline Baulant, Anton J. Schuurman, and Paul Servais, Actes du Séminaire Tenu dans le Cadre du 9ème Congrès International d'Histoire Économique de Berne (Louvain-la-Neuve, Belgium: Academia, 1988), 173. Consequently the interdependence of prices in an economy needs to be emphasized, especially as it affects historical commodity price indexes. For a direct test of the applicability of precisely the point made herein, see S[imon] D. Smith, 'Prices and the Value of English Exports in the Eighteenth Century: Evidence from the North American Colonial Trade,' *Economic History Review*, 2nd Ser., 48 (August 1995): 575–90.

Perhaps the most balanced and sensible comments in this whole matter are those of M[ichael] W. Flinn, 'Trends in Real Wages, 1750–1850,' *Economic History Review*, 2d Ser., 27 (August 1974): 402: 'Frail and inadequate as the existing indexes are, objections to them can, however, be taken too far. Nobody seriously expects indexes for periods as far back in time as this to be exact within a per cent or two.'

None of which is meant by any of the authors cited—and certainly not by the present writer—to deny that regional variations in prices can and did exist, if only because it took—and takes—time and money to move information from place to place, and it took—and takes—time and money to move goods from place to place. For a valuable discussion of spatial variations in prices in the late nineteenth century, see Michael R. Haines, 'A State and Local Consumer Price Index for the United States in 1890,' *Historical Methods: A Journal of Quantitative an Interdisciplinary History*, 22 (Summer 1989): 97–105.

pile a price relative series for each of the commodities and take the average of the several price relatives? Then, in considering the average to be calculated, the researcher needs to decide whether to compute an arithmetic mean or some other measure of central tendency, perhaps a geometric mean.

Again the availability of a great deal of data for the modern period has allowed index number theorists to test out all the various options. The consensus seems to be, first, that an index based on an arithmetic mean is to be preferred because the resulting series can be manipulated statistically more easily than one based on the alternatives and, second, that the aggregate or market basket index is to be preferred because it can more easily be recomputed to a new reference base number, thus facilitating comparisons. Nevertheless, as Irving Fisher wrote, 'from a practical standpoint, it is quite unnecessary to discuss the fanciful arguments for using "one formula for one purpose and another for another," in view of the great practical fact that all methods (if free of freakishness and bias) *agree!*'[19]

There are two types of general price indexes produced by these methods. The wholesale commodity price index and the retail commodity price index are intended to describe two different but closely associated sets of price movements in an economy. The former has sometimes been called, perhaps more accurately, the producer's price index in that it is an index of the prices of primary

19. Fisher, *Making of Index Numbers*, 231 (emphasis as in the original). Joseph A. Schumpeter, *History of Economic Analysis*, ed. [Romaine] Elizabeth Boody Schumpeter (New York: Oxford University Press, [1954]), 872, raised the possibility that 'some future historian may well consider [Fisher] . . . the greatest of America's scientific economists.' James Tobin, no mean scholar himself, acknowledged in his essay on Fisher in *The New Palgrave: A Dictionary of Economics*, ed. John Eatwell, Murray Milgate, and Peter Newman, 4 vols. (London: The Macmillan Press Ltd., 1987), 2:369: that 'Fisher is widely regarded as the greatest economist [the United States of] America has produced . . . America's first mathematical economist . . . the greatest expert of all time on index numbers.'
    Compare Hoover, 'Index Numbers: Practical Applications,' *International Encyclopedia of the Social Sciences*, ed. Sills, 7:159. Note in this regard Robert E. Gallman's discussion of papers by Terry L. Anderson and Allan [L.] Kullikoff in 'Comment,' *Journal of Economic History*, 39 (March 1979): 311–12. Compare Earl J. Hamilton, 'Prices, Wages, and the Industrial Revolution,' in *Studies in Economics and Industrial Relations*, ed. Wesley C. Mitchell et al. (Philadelphia: University of Pennsylvania Press, 1941), 102, n. 6.

market items. It is prone to more extreme fluctuations than the retail index, not only in the short run but also sometimes even over longer periods. The retail price index is better described as the index of prices paid by consumers, the commodity price index. It is also known as the cost of living index, reflecting a primary purpose in calculating it. Its movements are less volatile than those of the wholesale price index. This is the index more properly used to deflate such things as wage rate series in order to test the changes in the real purchasing power of wage earners (thus, 'real wages') or to deflate estate valuations to measure changes in real levels of wealth.

Those who construct historical price indexes, while ideally using retail prices, are sometimes faced with the necessity of turning to wholesale prices. Once again we can find reassurance in the knowledge that both types of indexes are and were highly correlated. Where we have the opportunity of checking, the two indexes generally move in the same direction and change directions at the same time. The results of such compromises, born of necessity and indicated herein by the use of the phrase 'commodity price index,' are, consequently, reasonably satisfactory.[20]

'Satisfactory for what purpose?' the reader may ask. Economists, historians, and economic historians have turned price indexes to two purposes. First, and most important, commodity price indexes have been used to trace and analyze the movement of prices across time. The commodity price index itself allows us to describe the trend in, the cycles in, and even the seasonal variations in the average levels of prices, the last provided we have monthly or quarterly data. It is also possible to utilize a commodity price index to help make better sense out of the history of the price of a single commodity. Changes in the price of each commodity have both common causes and more specific causes.

20. For an especially germane discussion of this matter, see Paul A. David and Peter Solar, 'A Bicentenary Contribution to the History of the Cost of Living in America,' *Research in Economic History*, 2 (1977): 1–80, esp. 15–17, 40–57. Compare Flinn, 'Trends in Real Wages,' 402: 'In the long run, and in many cases even in the short run, retail prices must move in sympathy with wholesale prices.'

Deflating a price series of an individual commodity using the commodity price index in effect filters out what was happening generally —those conditions that affected all commodities—and effectively places in relief just what was particular to the price history of a specific commodity. In a similar fashion, we may use the commodity price index to deflate other economic series such as import and export data, wage rates, national product figures, and so forth, in order to understand better the real directions that they took, regardless of changes in the money in which they were measured.

It should be obvious that there are dangers inherent in any simple cross-temporal or cross-cultural comparisons that fail to pay full regard to context. For instance, an annual income of $25,000 in the United States today and an equivalent amount in, say, contemporary India may mean considerably different things in terms of the earner's relative standard of living, social status, perhaps even political orientation.[21] Similar difficulties arise with comparisons over time and, indeed, are even more of a problem for being less obvious as well as for involving the technical problems of constructing indexes that accurately reflect real price changes. A question about the worth of something has much more than just a mathematical answer.[22]

21. 'That even the best index numbers designed to measure changes in the purchasing power of money have numerous philosophical and mathematical defects every economist knows. *The purchasing power of money* is difficult to conceive and still more difficult to measure even within the limits of definite assumptions about the meaning of the term' (Hamilton, 'Use and Misuse of Price History,' 49 [emphasis as in the original]). Compare Irving B. Kravis, 'Comparative Studies of National Incomes and Prices,' *Journal of Economic Literature*, 22 (March 1984): 1–39; W[alter] E. Diewert, 'Index Numbers,' in *New Palgrave*, eds. Eatwell, Milgate and Newman, 2:767–80; and the essays in Wolfgang Eichhorn, *Measurement in Economics: Theory and Application of Economic Indices* (Heidelberg: Physica-Verlag, 1988), esp. 49–164. See also Irving Fisher and Harry G. Brown, *The Purchasing Power of Money: Its Determination and Relation to Credit, Interest, and Crises*, rev. ed. (New York: Macmillan, 1922).

22. There is consistent concern about these difficulties among the compilers of the indexes themselves. See, for instance, Franklin M. Fisher and Karl Shell, 'Taste and Quality Change in the Pure Theory of the True Cost-of-Living Index,' in *Value, Capital, and Growth: Papers in Honour of Sir John Hicks*, ed. J[ames] N. Wolfe (Edinburgh: Edinburgh University Press, 1967), 97–139; and the essays and the items in the bibliography in *Price Indexes and Quality Change: Studies in New Methods of Measurement*, ed. Zvi Griliches (Cambridge: Harvard University Press, 1971). It is these debates to which David and Solar, 'Cost of Living,' 4–5, refer in their discussion of the dissatisfactions of neoclassical econo-

The most important ramification of the greater attention to and application of commodity price indexes as a measure of changing price levels has been in the arena of public policy. We of the early twenty-first century await the monthly release of the latest commodity price index numbers with some trepidation, having been taught to read them as one of the vital signs of the economy. Nations with high rates of inflation are thought to be 'problem economies,' while the economies of nations with low rates of inflation are considered sounder.[23] Governments with 'problem economies' continue to be under considerable political pressure from a concerned populace to reduce inflation.[24] One solution to inflation has been the use of commodity price indexes to 'index' such things as workers' salaries, to protect payments under government social programs, and to develop government-subsidized investment plans to make investments in them 'inflation proof.'[25] The commodity price index over the last two centuries

———

mists with traditional, classical formulations of commodity price indexes. See also Melville J. Ulmer, *The Economic Theory of Cost of Living Index Numbers* (New York: Columbia University Press, 1949); Robert A. Pollak, *The Theory of the Cost-of-Living Index* (New York: Oxford University Press, 1989); and Mark A. Wynne and Fiona D. Sigalla, 'The Consumer Price Index,' *Economic Review — Federal Reserve Bank of Dallas*, [74] (Second Quarter, 1994), 1–22. See especially the 1996 report of the Boskin Commission and the related symposium it engendered as published in the *Journal of Economic Perspectives*, 12 (Winter 1998): 3–78.

Economic historians, who should not only be more sensitive than others to the complexities of such comparisons but also be better suited to deal with them, are in fact guilty of some of the most simplistic, even misleading use of price indexes. One economic historian who has explored the issues carefully is Alice Hanson Jones, *American Colonial Wealth: Documents and Methods for the American Middle Colonies*, 1774, a separate number of *Economic Development and Cultural Change*, 18 (July 1970): 124–40. See also, Lindert, 'Probates, Prices, and Preindustrial Living Standards,' 175–76.

23. A moderate rate of inflation is indeed thought good for an economy because it contributes to the generation of additional output and employment. In such circumstances, as David Hume wrote, 'labour and industry gain life; the merchant becomes more enterprising, the manufacturer more diligent and skilful, and even the farmer follows his plough with greater alacrity and attention.' See his essay 'On Money,' one of his *Political Discourses* (Edinburgh: A. Kincaid and A. Donaldson, 1752), as reprinted in Hume, *Essays, Moral, Political, and Literary*, ed. Eugene F. Miller, rev. ed. (Indianapolis, Ind.: Liberty Classics, 1985), 281–94 (quot., p. 286).

24. Consider, as one example only, the ongoing debate in Britain over the rate of inflation and the country's entry into the European Monetary System. See B. M. Craven and R. Gausden, 'How Best to Measure Inflation? The UK and Europe,' *The Royal Bank of Scotland Review*, No. 170 (June 1991): 26–37. Compare Roger Bootle, *The Death of Inflation: Surviving & Thriving in the Zero Era*, [2nd ed.] (London: Nicholas Brealey, 1997).

25. See [United States, Department of Labor, Bureau of Labor Statistics], *BLS Handbook*

has developed from a novel technique for validating price comparisons into a central element of public policy planning.

The second purpose to which commodity price indexes have been turned is one for which they were not designed and are not necessarily very well suited, but a purpose which nevertheless has been sanctioned by long usage. We frequently see the fluctuations in a commodity price index discussed and displayed as if they described the fluctuations in the performance of an economy, as if the commodity price index ran parallel to the movement of the gross domestic product or were some sort of surrogate for it.[26] No one would deny that the two are interrelated if only because the prevailing price level and the performance of the economy as a whole reflect many of the same phenomena. Yet neither would anyone who has lived in the United States over the past generation or two, or in any other country during a period of 'stagflation,' necessarily equate rising prices with a 'good' economy. If

_____

of Methods, Bureau of Labor Statistics, Bulletin 2285 (Washington, D.C.: United States Government Printing Office, 1988), 157. Compare several of the papers in *Stabilization of the Domestic and International Economy*, ed. Karl Brunner and Allan H. Meltzer, Carnegie-Rochester Conference Series on Public Policy, Vol. 5 (Amsterdam: North-Holland Publishing Company, 1977).

26. It is a practice particularly popular with journalists and writers of textbooks. See, e.g., Gilbert C. Fite and Jim E. Reese, *An Economic History of the United States*, 3rd ed. (Boston: Houghton Mifflin Co., 1973), 160–61; Harold Underwood Faulkner, *American Economic History*, rev. by Harry N. Scheiber and Harold G. Vatter, 9th ed. (New York: Harper & Row, [1976]), 8–11; Paul A. Samuelson and William D. Nordhaus, *Economics*, 12th ed. (New York: McGraw-Hill Book Co., 1985), end papers, table 'National Output and Price Levels during the Twentieth Century'; and Jonathan [R. T.] Hughes, *American Economic History*, 3rd. ed. (Glenview, Ill.: Scott, Foresman and Co., 1990). Hughes states (p. 216): 'In an economy as free to respond to the signals of the market as was the antebellum economy [of the United States], general price movements indicate changes in the pace of economic life *in a rough way*' (emphasis as in the original). Compare Richard B. Morris, ed., *Encyclopedia of American History*, rev. ed. (New York: Harper & Row, 1965), 536–41. W[alt] W. Rostow and Michael Kennedy, 'A Simple Model of the Kondratieff Cycle,' *Research in Economic History*, 4 (1979): 1–36, offer an explanation as to why this was so. Compare Michael D. Bordo and Anna J. Schwartz, 'Money and Prices in the 19th Century: Was Thomas Tooke Right?' *Explorations in Economic History*, 18 (April 1981): 97–127. See also Geoffrey H. Moore, 'A Truism: Recession Slows Inflation,' *New York Times*, Sunday, November 18, 1979, Business and Finance section. For evidence that this did not work all of the time, see Herbert S. Klein and Stanley L. Engerman, 'Methods and Meanings in Price History,' in *Essays on the Price History of Eighteenth-Century Latin America*, edited by Lyman L. Johnson and Enrique Tandeter (Albuquerque, N.M.: University of New Mexico Press, [1990]), 15 and passim.

anything, as was mentioned just above, today, when we view the commodity price index as one of the vital signs of the economy, the correlation we draw may be just the reverse of the relationship implied in this use of the commodity price index by economic historians. Nevertheless, the argument can be made that stagflation is a new economic phenomenon and that, at least until the middle of the twentieth century, periods of rising prices generally corresponded well with periods of economic growth just as periods of falling prices were periods of economic decline. In other words, we can agree that cycles in price levels paralleled the business cycle.[27] Economic historians have indeed accepted this proposition and have relied on commodity price indexes to chart the course of the economy at least down to the time of the Great Depression and the New Deal (see fig.1).[28]

27. 'Price levels . . . may be a fairly inexact index of swings of the business cycle, but for many centuries they have to suffice.' [Thomas C. Cochran], 'A Survey of Concepts and Viewpoints in the Social Sciences,' in *The Social Sciences in Historical Study: A Report of the Committee on Historiography*, [ed. Hugh G. J. Aitken], Social Science Research Council, Bulletin 64 (New York: Social Science Research Council, 1965), 85. Or, to quote Arthur F. Burns and Wesley C. Mitchell: 'Indexes of wholesale prices have served more faithfully as "barometers" of business cycles than many students now believe.' (Burns and Mitchell, *Measuring Business Cycles*, National Bureau of Economic Research, Studies in Business Cycles, Vol. 2 (New York: National Bureau of Economic Research, 1946): 75.) They date the divergence in the relationship between the two as beginning with the 1920s and 1930s. Compare Victor Zarnowitz and Geoffrey H. Moore, 'Major Changes in Cyclical Behavior,' in *The American Business Cycle: Continuity and Change*, ed. Robert J. Gordon, National Bureau of Economic Research, Studies in Business Cycles, Vol. 25 (Chicago: University of Chicago Press, 1986): 554–55, and, especially, the papers by Robert E. Lucas, Jr., 'Understanding Business Cycles,' in *Stabilization of the Domestic and International Economy*, ed. Brunner and Meltzer, 7–29, and by Finn E. Kydland and Edward C. Prescott, 'Business Cycles: Real Facts and a Monetary Myth,' *Federal Reserve Bank of Minneapolis Quarterly Review*, 14 (Spring 1990): 3–18. For a wider introduction to the subject, see Thomas E. Hall, *Business Cycles: The Nature and Causes of Economic Fluctuations* (New York: Praeger Publishers, 1990). The post-1930s counter-cyclical character of price movements is not unique to the economy of the United States. See David K. Backus and Patrick J. Kehoe, 'International Evidence on the Historical Properties of Business Cycles,' *American Economic Review*, 82 (September 1992): 864–88. See also *Business Cycles and Depressions: An Encyclopedia*, ed. David Glasner (New York: Garland Publishing, 1997). Nevertheless, Geoffrey Moore could write as late as 1977 that one of the 'little known facts about inflation' is that it 'is closely tied to the business cycle. . . . Every downturn in the business cycle since 1948 has been associated with a downturn in the rate of inflation, and every upturn in the business cycle has been accompanied by an upturn in the rate of inflation, measured by the consumer price index (CPI).' Moore, *Business Cycles, Inflation, and Forecasting* (Cambridge, Mass.: National Bureau of Economic Research, 1980), 209.
28. This includes using them to identify the cycles of the early United States economy

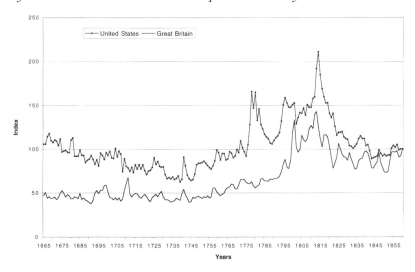

Fig. 1. Commodity Price Indexes, United States and Great Britain, 1665–1860. (Base: 1860=100.)

While it is certainly necessary that any who turn to a commodity price index be alert to all of these questions, at least in the very broad terms outlined here, we need not worry ourselves with the details of their construction or application in order to employ them for good purposes. Economic historians of the modern period are fortunate in that other scholars, better equipped than they to deal with these matters, have largely sorted out the issues and have already provided us with several good price indexes. This is particularly the case for the United States for the period from the late eighteenth century to the present (see Appendix A).

The primary purpose of this monograph is the presentation of a consistent commodity price index that extends across as much as

(see Appendix E, below). For evidence of the existence of the business cycle as a persistent feature of the economy over the centuries, see Raymond [A.] De Roover, *The Medici Bank: Its Organization, Management, Operations, and Decline* (New York: New York University Press, 1948), 48–49. For cycles in the economy of Great Britain, see Appendix D, below.

possible of the history of the United States. A general discussion
of commodity price indexes precedes an examination and evaluation of various previously constructed series. Table A-1 displays
some of them, links them, and brings them up to date. The text
discusses several issues raised by that compilation. The effort is
consummated in the summary index presented in Table A-1, Column 6. It is complemented by both an explanation of how to compute price comparisons over time using the index number series
as a general price deflator and by the presentation of some examples of such calculations, especially as they apply to data from the
seventeenth and eighteenth centuries.

As one example from the twentieth century, consider that an
economist wants to know how many 1987 dollars it would take to
buy a house priced at $10,000 in 1953. To do so, he or she has
simply to turn to a table such as Table A-1 where, in Column 6,
one finds the commodity price index numbers for the two years in
question and then calculates the ratio between them.[29] Using that
ratio as a multiplier, one can ascertain that, if the cost of housing
had increased over the years to the same extent as all commodity
prices, a house priced at $10,000 in 1953 should have cost roughly
$42,500 in 1987 dollars.[30]

The computation is easy; the answer is mathematically sound;
but the qualifying word 'roughly' is all-important. The result of

---

29. Computation: The index number for 1953 is 320; the number for 1987 is 1,359. The
ratio between 1,359 and 320 is 4.25 (1,359 ÷ 320 = 4.25).
   To avoid any impression of precision in the results of calculations that are inherently im-
precise, numbers expressed in the text throughout this study are rounded upwards. In
rounding, when the number to the right is a '5,' the value to the left is raised if it is an odd
number (55 is stated as 60) and not raised if it is an even number (65 is stated as 60).
   30. Computation: 10,000 x 4.25 = 42,500. Note that, in reversing the procedure, the ratio is employed as a divisor rather than a multiplier. Thus $42,500 in 1987 terms, divided
by 4.25, equals $10,000 in 1953 terms. If one wishes to reduce several figures to a common
denominator, a different procedure is required. It is possible, e.g., to state the values from
both years in terms of 1860 dollars simply by dividing the two amounts by the index numbers for the respective years (1953 and 1987). It is necessary always to remember that the
index number is in fact a percentage and, before using it as a divisor, to express it as such.
Thus one divides 42,500 by 13.59 and 10,000 by 3.2. The quotient in both divisions is, of
course, the same figure. The house was worth about $3,100 in 1860 dollars—if the cost of
housing had increased over the years to the same extent as all commodity prices.

such a calculation is better considered as hypothetical rather than as definitive. In fact, because housing costs actually grew faster than the average level of prices over the intervening three decades by some 31 percent, the kind of house that cost $10,000 in 1953 really cost about $55,000 in 1987.[31] The lesson—that housing costs outran the average level of prices over the three decades—is valuable not only because it illustrates one of the potential problems implicit in such comparisons but also because it shows the kinds of insights to be gained from their careful use. The commodity price index describes merely the central tendency in the movement of prices of all commodities.

Historians interested in the period before the American Revolutionary War do basically the same calculations, although with one additional step, and they must be even more cautious in their conclusions because of the much longer time span involved. Before the introduction of the dollar as the money of account of the new nation, each colony had its own currency—all denominated in pounds, shillings, and pence, and each used the same counting system, the same abbreviations and money symbols. The pound sign was '£'; 's' was the abbreviation for the shilling; and a 'd'— from *denarius*, the Latin word for penny—stood for a penny or pence. A pound contained twenty shillings, and a shilling contained twelve pennies. (These were written as £1 = 20s and 1s = 12d [∴ £1 = 240d].)[32]

Because the commodity price indexes discussed herein are ex-

31. [United States, President], *Economic Report of the President . . . 1990* (Washington, D.C.: United States Government Printing Office, 1990), 360. Compare the debate over the impact of housing costs on the British measure of inflation. See Craven and Gausden, 'How Best to Measure Inflation?', 26–37.

32. The origins of this scheme go back at least as far as the middle of the eighth century, prior to the era of King Charlemagne. Philip Grierson, 'Money and Coinage under Charlemagne,' in *Karl der Grosse: Lebenswerk und Nachleben*, ed. Wolfgang Braunfels et al., [3rd ed.], 5 vols. (Düsseldorf: L. Schwann, [1967–1968]), 3:501: 'The silver coins were known as pennies or deniers (*denarii*) and were reckoned 12 to the shilling or sou (*solidus*) and 240 to the pound or livre (*libra*). . . .' Twelve centuries later, monetary reform, introduced into Great Britain as of February 15, 1971, decimalized the currency, did away with the shilling, and introduced both 'new pence' (£1 = 100p) as a money of account and new coins as well. See the Decimal Currency Act, 1967, Act of Elizabeth II, 1967, c. 47; and the Decimal Currency Act, 1969, Act of Elizabeth II, 1969, c. 19. References in this format to

pressed in dollars, historians must first convert any seventeenth-
or eighteenth-century prices from pounds to dollars. This is most
easily accomplished by changing an amount in colonial currency
to its equivalent in pounds sterling and then going from pounds
sterling to dollars at the standard seventeenth- and eighteenth-
century ratio of 4s 6d sterling per dollar. For example, in 1774,
when the exchange rate was £135 Massachusetts currency per
£100 sterling, £400 Massachusetts currency was equivalent to
£296 sterling. (For the rate of exchange, see Table B-1, below.) At
£0.225 sterling per dollar, or, inversely, $4.44 per one pound ster-
ling, £296 sterling was equal to $1,314.[33] The two index numbers
from Table A-1, Column 6, for 1774 and 2000, are, respectively,
97 and 2,059; the ratio between them is twenty-one to one; and
£400 Massachusetts currency in 1774, when adjusted for
inflation, works out to have been worth about $28,000 United
States currency in the year 2000. (Compare Table 1.)[34]

Using the explanation just given, it is possible for anyone to
convert any sum in colonial currency to its approximate dollar
amount today. Table 1 shows several additional examples derived
in the same manner and serves as a means of extending the discussion a bit further. For six colonies, for four periods of peace in
the eighteenth century each of them spanning a full economic cycle from peak to peak,[35] Table 1 gives the value in year 2000 dol-

---

British laws from the last century and a half can be traced in [Great Britain, Laws and
Statutes], *The Public General Acts* (London: Her Majesty's Stationery Office, 1831 to date).
For these two statutes, see *Public General Acts . . . , 1967*, 1:1019–26 (1967 c. 47); *Public Gen-
eral Acts . . . , 1969*, 1:151–74 (1969 c. 19).

33. It is better to do the calculation in this way, than to try to go from colonial pounds
directly to dollars, because the ratio between dollars (pieces of eight) and sterling stayed
the same over the seventeenth and eighteenth centuries and is known, while the ratio between dollars and each colonial currency varied considerably and is less well known. The
availability of currency-to-sterling exchange rates—as in Table B-1, below—makes such calculations relatively easy. The traditional expression of sterling in pounds, shillings and
pence is here converted to decimalized format (£1 = 100p) for ease of calculation. For example, 4s 6d is rendered £0.225 or 22.5p.Cf. McCusker, *Money and Exchange in Europe and America*, 323. For the par value of the dollar and the pound sterling, see Appendix C, n. 17, below.

34. Computation: 2,059 ÷ 97 = 21; 1,314 x 21 = 27,594.

35. Following Bishop Fleetwood's dictum that '. . . you must never take a very dear year,
to your prejudice, nor a very cheap one, in your favour, nor indeed any single year, to be

TABLE I

THE EQUIVALENT IN YEAR 2000 UNITED STATES DOLLARS
TO £100 LOCAL CURRENCY
FOR SIX OF THE CONTINENTAL COLONIES
FROM FOUR PERIODS IN THE EIGHTEENTH CENTURY

	In the Years			
	1713–1719	1727–1738	1766–1772	1782–1796
	1	2	3	4
£100 *Massachusetts Colonial Currency*				
At a Sterling Exchange Rate of	£173.26	£368.94	£131.46	
Was Equivalent at That Time to	$256.51	$120.46	$338.09	$333.33
Is Roughly Equivalent in Year 2000$ to	$6,700.00	$3,400.00	$7,200.00	$5,600.00
£100 *New York Colonial Currency*				
At a Sterling Exchange Rate of	£155.84	£165.16	£175.15	
Was Equivalent at That Time to	$285.19	$269.10	$253.74	$250.00
Is Roughly Equivalent in Year 2000$ to	$7,400.00	$7,700.00	$5,400.00	$4,200.00
£100 *Pennsylvania Colonial Currency*				
At a Sterling Exchange Rate of	£132.82	£159.66	£162.01	
Was Equivalent at That Time to	$334.63	$278.38	$274.34	$266.67
Is Roughly Equivalent in Year 2000$ to	$8,700.00	$7,900.00	$5,800.00	$4,400.00
£100 *Maryland Colonial Currency*				
At a Sterling Exchange Rate of	£133.33	£134.33	£160.81	
Was Equivalent at That Time to	$333.34	$330.86	$276.38	$266.67
Is Roughly Equivalent in Year 2000$ to	$8,700.00	$9,400.00	$5,900.00	$4,400.00
£100 *Virginia Colonial Currency*				
At a Sterling Exchange Rate of	£108.50	£120.59	£123.74	
Was Equivalent at That Time to	$409.63	$368.55	$359.18	$333.33
Is Roughly Equivalent in Year 2000$ to	$10,700.00	$10,500.00	$7,600.00	$5,600.00
£100 *South Carolina Colonial Currency*				
At a Sterling Exchange Rate of	£346.32	£718.95	£696.57	
Was Equivalent at That Time to	$128.33	$61.82	$63.86	$428.57
Is Roughly Equivalent in Year 2000$ to	$3,300.00	$1,800.00	$1,400.00	$7,100.00

NOTES AND SOURCES: Shown are the equivalent values of £100 local, colonial currency in both contemporary dollars and in year 2000 dollars for four periods in the eighteenth century. The dates shown in the column headings are those of four periods of peace over a full business cycle or two (peak to peak). The cycles are identified in Table E-1. The sterling exchange rates are the average annual rates over each period and are expressed as the amount of colonial currency equal to £100 sterling. For the exchange rates, see Table B-1, below. For Massachusetts, Columns 1 and 2 are in Old Tenor and Column 3 is in Lawful Money. For Maryland, the figures are in Hard Currency. Because we lack adequate exchange rate data for Maryland for the first period, these calculations used the par of exchange instead (133.33). See John J. McCusker, *Money and Exchange in Europe and America, 1600–1775: A Handbook* (2d ed.; Chapel Hill: University of North Carolina Press, [1992]), 131–37, 189–96. The dollar amounts in Column 4 for 1782–96 (for South Carolina, 1783–96; see Appendix C, below) are at the set ratios that applied after the American Revolutionary War as discussed in Appendix C. The year 2000 dollar equivalencies to the £100 currency figures are derived using the index numbers in Table A-1, Column 6, and the method described above in the text.

lars of £100 in each of the local, colonial currencies. We can see that, for example, on the average over the years 1766–72, £100 Pennsylvania currency was roughly the value of $5,800 in 2000 terms. By extension, £10 Pennsylvania currency would be worth about $580 and £1 currency $58. Given the counting system in use in Great Britain and its colonies, we can suggest that, on the eve of the American Revolutionary War, one shilling in Pennsylvania currency was worth around $2.90 in 2000 dollars and one penny, about 24 cents.[36]

Comparisons of amounts from several different periods combine the methods used in the calculations outlined above. Thus, it is possible to determine the comparative worth of the legacies of two individuals whose estates were probated, for example, in Massachusetts in 1755 and 1855. Let us say that the first estate was inventoried at £1,750 Massachusetts currency; the second, at $1,750. To start, the first sum needs to be converted into dollars before it can be compared with the second one. In 1755, £1,750 Massachusetts currency was equivalent to £1,312 sterling and, therefore, $5,825.[37] From Table A-1, Column 6, where the index numbers for 1755 and 1855 are 79 and 104, respectively, and the one for the year 2000 is 2,059, we can determine that $5,825 in 1755 was equal in value to about $150,000 in year 2000 dollars and that $1,750 in 1855 was equivalent to $35,000 in 2000 dol-

your rule, but you must take the price . . . for as many years as you can. . . .' Fleetwood, *Chronicon Preciosum*, 135–36. The dating of the cycles is as they are identified in Table E-1. Compare S[imon] D. Smith, 'The Market for Manufactures in the Thirteen Continental Colonies, 1698–1776,' *Economic History Review*, [2nd ser.], 51 (November 1998): 706, who adds to the usual periods of warfare that had an impact on the colonial economy during the eighteenth century—those associated with colonial involvement in the Second Hundred Years' War between England and France (1702–13, 1739–48, 1754–63, 1775–83)—the years 1718–20, the Austro-Spanish War of 1717–20 that England joined in 1718. One might also note the brief Anglo-Spanish War of 1727–28. Neither of them had much impact in the Western Hemisphere, however.

36. The sharp-eyed reader will notice that these amounts are quite a bit more than the ones calculated for the first edition of this book, even across a short period of low levels of inflation.

37. Computation: With reference to Table B-1, we can determine that, in 1755 the Massachusetts currency to sterling exchange rate was 133.33. Thus £1,750 Massachusetts currency was worth £1,312 sterling. At 4.44 dollars per £1 sterling, £1,312 was the equivalent of $5,825 (1,312 x 4.44 = 5,825).

lars.[38] In real terms, the former estate was worth well over four times the value of the latter one.

The appearance of precision in all of these exercises, and, indeed, their inviting simplicity, should not obscure two important realities. We would be fortunate indeed if the data were good enough to allow us to be within 10 percent of the true mathematical figure, plus or minus, meaning, for instance, that we can expect the worth of £100 Pennsylvania currency over 1766–72 to be in the range of $5,200 to $6,400 (2000 dollars).[39] Although it is cleaner and computationally much more convenient to use a mean rather than a range, we need to remember that the mathematical mean merely designates the central tendency within a range. Nevertheless, as Paul David and Peter Solar suggest, 'consumer price indices of the familiar kind presented here . . . are capable of being given a reasonably precise economic interpretation.'[40] Even more significantly, we should always remind ourselves that the mathematical answer to our question may not address all of the important issues. To repeat my refrain: 'A question about the worth of something has much more than just a mathematical answer.' As with all other pieces of historical evidence, before drawing any conclusions, we need to evaluate it in context, and weigh its implications in time and place. The commodity price index as a deflator of money amounts over time is a tool, the 'real value' a means to an interpretative end, and never the answer in itself.

And what, then, about the questions posed at the beginning of this exercise? President Washington in 1795, early in his second

38. Computation: The ratio between 79 and 2,059 is 26.1 and between 104 and 2,059 is 19.8. As before, these ratios are employed as multipliers applied to each of the respective dollar amounts and, consequently $5,825 is seen to have been the equivalent of about $150,000 (5,825 x 26.1 = 152,032) and $1,750 is seen to have been the equivalent of about $34,000 (1,750 x 19.8 = 34,650).

39. See in this regard Eric E. Lampard's suggestion as repeated by Sam Bass Warner, Jr., *Writing Local History: The Use of Social Statistics*, Technical Leaflet 7, rev. ed. (Nashville, Tennessee: American Association for State and Local History, 1970), 4. Compare the comment by M. W. Flinn quoted in text, n. 18, above.

40. David and Solar, 'Cost of Living,' 2.

term of office, paid his dentist $60.00 for what seems likely to have been a new set of false teeth. When adjusted for inflation, $60.00 in 1795 terms was the equivalent of roughly $820 in year 2000 terms.[41] The gold doubloon to which eagle-eyed Tashtego earned a claim, 'the riveted gold coin' of Spanish colonial origins that passed current, as Melville tells us, for $16.00 in the United States in 1854, the year Melville published *Moby Dick*, was roughly the equivalent of $330 at the dawn of the twenty-first century—certainly not a whale of a lot of money, given the consequences.[42]

41. Washington, at Philadelphia, to John Greenwood, at New York, February 20, 1795, as printed in *The Writings of George Washington*, ed. John C. Fitzpatrick, 39 vols. (Washington, D.C.: United States Government Printing Office, [1931–1944]), 34:120–21. Given Washington's extreme reticence on the subject, even in his correspondence with his dentist, and given that there are gaps in the surviving exchanges of letters, we cannot be sure just what he was paying for on any given occasion. Over the decade of the 1790s Washington sent $15.00 or $20.00 to Greenwood several times for repair work. The 'Sixty dollars in Bank notes of the United States' is exceptional and thus seems to have been for a new set of teeth. I am grateful to the staff of The Papers of George Washington—the project that is overseeing the publication of those papers—for their help in locating and sending me copies of all such correspondence. I am particularly beholden to Dr. Dorothy Twohig, the project's editor-in-chief.

42. Herman Melville, *Moby-Dick or The Whale* (1851), ed. Harrison Hayford, G[eorge] Thomas Tanselle, and Hershel Parker, Vol. 6 of The Writings of Herman Melville: The Northwestern-Newberry Edition (Evanston and Chicago, Illinois: Northwestern University Press and The Newberry Library, 1988), 160–61, 430–35, 547, 564, 791, 893–94. For the doubloon—the 'doblon de á ocho escudos' or the quadruple *pistole*—see Robert Chalmers, *A History of Currency in the British Colonies* (London: Her Majesty's Stationery Office, [1893]), 106, 395–96, 407. One *escudo* in gold equaled by definition two silver dollars, so, as Melville wrote, the doubloon was worth $16.00. See also the table in Figure C-2, below. Compare Jürgen Schneider et al., *Währungen der Welt*, 14 pts, in 11 vols., Beiträge zur Wirtschafts- und Sozialgeschichte, Nos. 44–50, 57, 59, 61 (Stuttgart: Franz Steiner, 1991–1996), 1, pt. i: 233. Foreign gold and silver coins circulated legally in the United States at rates set in the 'Act Regulating Foreign Coins, and For Other Purposes,' February 9, 1793, ch. 5, and in subsequent legislation, most notably the 'Act Regulating the Value of Certain Foreign Gold Coins within the United States,' June 28, 1834, ch. 96, until a new law—the 'Act Relating to Foreign Coins and to the Coinage of Cents at the Mint of the United States,' February 21, 1857, ch. 56—withdrew their legal tender status. This effectively outlawed the use of foreign coinage. See [United States, Laws and Statutes], *The Statutes at Large of the United States of America*, ed. Richard Peters, George Minot, and George P. Sanger, 17 vols. (Boston: Little, Brown and Company, 1845–73), 1:300–1, 4:700–1, 11:163–64. Compare Oscar G. Schilke and Raphael E. Solomon, *America's Foreign Coins: An Illustrated Standard Catalogue with Valuations of Foreign Coins with Legal Tender Status in the United States, 1793–1857* (New York: Coin and Currency Institute, 1964), 188 et passim. See also David A. Martin, 'The Changing Role of Foreign Money in the United States, 1782–1857,' *Journal of Economic History*, 37 (December 1977): 1009–27.

Examples of Calculations

Example 1

Question: How much is £750 Pennsylvania currency in 1750 worth today?

Solution

Step One: Reduce £750 Pennsylvania currency to pounds sterling.

Have reference to Table B-1, where the exchange rate between pounds currency and pounds sterling for 1750 is shown to be £170.65 Pennsylvania currency per £100 sterling. Thus £750 currency is £440 sterling (750 ÷ 1.7065 = 439.5).

Step Two: Convert £440 sterling into dollars.

Given that £1 sterling was the equivalent of $4.44, £440 sterling was worth $1,951 (439.5 x 4.44 = 1951.4).

Step Three: Find the equivalent of $1,951 1750 dollars in dollars of the year 2000.

From Table A-1, determine that the commodity price index number for 1750 is 84 and for 2000 is 2,059. The ratio between the two numbers is 25 (2,059 ÷ 84 = 25). Multiply the number of 1750 dollars by the ratio (1,951.4 x 25 = 47,815).

Answer: The sum of £750 Pennsylvania currency in 1750 is roughly equivalent to $48,000 in the year 2000.

Example 2

The Issue: In the spring of 1789, Gillespie Birney and Company offered 'ten Guineas' reward for money stolen from its 'store house' in Danville, Kentucky, earlier that same year. The thief made off with 'Cash to the amount of seventy pound Virginia currency, amongst which was five Doubloons, and two German Carolines, which was remarkable.'[43]

Question: What portion of the total amount stolen was in doubloons and carolines, how big was the reward compared with the amount stolen, and how much was all this worth today?

Solution

Step One: Reduce the various amounts to dollars.

43. *Kentucky Gazette* (Lexington), April 4, 1789. The theft occurred in the evening of January 24th.

The total value of the coins and, presumably, paper money stolen amounted to £70 Virginia currency, the money of account in use in what was then still part of the state of Virginia.

With reference to Appendix C and the table in Figure C-2, see that £1 Virginia currency was worth a set rate of $3.33\frac{1}{3}$ in the 1780s and after. Thus £70 currency was equivalent to $233.33 (3.33 x 70 = 233).

The three types of coins mentioned—British guineas, German carolines, and Spanish doubloons—were all gold coins worth, respectively, in Virginia currency, £1 8s 0d, £1 8s 0d and £4 8s 0d each.[44] Thus ten guineas were worth £14 Virginia currency, or $46.67, and the five doubloons and two carolines worth £24 16s 0d, or $82.67.

Step Two: Find the equivalent of $233 in 1789 dollars in dollars of the year 2000.

From Table A-1 ascertain that the commodity price index number for 1789 is 106 and for 2000 is 2,059. The ratio between the two numbers is 19.4 (2,059 ÷ 106 = 19.4). Multiply the number of 1789 dollars by the ratio (233 x 19.4 = 4,527).

Answer: The seven stolen gold coins, $82.67 out of a total of $233.33, constituted about 35 percent of the total. The reward—at $46.67—was precisely 20 percent of the total. The sum of £70 Virginia currency in 1788 is roughly equivalent to $4,500 in the year 2000.

What was likely to have been thought 'remarkable' in all this was the proportion of the total in gold coins rather than the presence of two German gold coins as part of the hoard.

---

44. For the guinea, see Figure 2. For the caroline, see Figure 3. The guinea was an English gold coin minted from 1663 to 1813, originally for use in the trade with Africa (thus the name). From 1717 on it was fixed in value at 21s and, at that value, continued to be referenced as a money of account into the last third of the twentieth century. The 'caroline,' or 'Carolin d'Or,' was a gold coin issued by Austrian and German states in the 1730s: among the former, the County of Montfort (see the carolins of Count Anton III [issued 1734–1736]); among the latter, the Duchy of Bavaria (see the carolins of Duke Karl Albrecht [issued 1726–1737]), the state of Hesse-Darmstadt (see the carolin of Landgrave Ernst Ludwig [issued 1733]), and the Duchy of Württemberg (see the carolins of Duke Eberhard Ludwig [issued 1731–1733] and Duke Karl Alexander [issued 1734–1736]). See Chester L. Krause and Clifford Mishler, *Standard Catalog of World Coins: Eighteenth Century, 1701–1800*, 2nd ed. ([Isola, Wisconsin: Krause Publications, 1997]), 90, 266, 377, 554. These coins were roughly equivalent to the guinea. They were circulating in the colonies at that rate by 1750. *A Pocket Almanack for the Year 1751. Fitted to the Use of Pennsylvania, and All the Neighbouring Provinces* (Philadelphia, Pennsylvania: B[enjamin] Franklin and D[avid] Hall, [1750]), [24]. In the notice by the newly organized—if unchartered—Bank of New-York of its 'Rules,' published in the *New York Packet*, June 7, 1784, it rated the guinea at $4.67 and the caroline at $4.75. At that rate carolines were worth £1 8s 6d Virginia currency. For the value of these coins, see also the table in Figure C-2.

Fig. 2. A Guinea, Great Britain, 1761 (obverse). Thomas Snelling, *A View of the Coins at This Time Current Throughout Europe* (London: T[homas] Snelling, 1766), plate 1.

Fig. 3. A Caroline, Hesse-Darmstadt, 1733 (obverse). Showing the mark of mint master 'G[eorg Christoph] K[uster].' Thomas Snelling, *A View of the Coins at This Time Current Throughout Europe* (London: T[homas] Snelling, 1766), plate 7. Courtesy, Baker Library, Harvard Business School.

APPENDIX A

COMMODITY PRICE INDEXES, UNITED STATES, 1665–2000

THE WORK OF MANY in compiling commodity price indexes for the United States was summarized, reviewed, and amplified in a 1976 paper by two economists, Peter Solar and Paul A. David. The essence of their careful construction of an index of consumer prices in the United States over the previous two hundred years was their Table 1 entitled 'Index of Consumer Prices, 1774–1974'; they referred to that series as the Brady/David/Solar index in recognition of their dependence on the estimates of Dorothy Brady, a label that will be replicated herein; their data are reproduced below in Column 3 of Table A-1.[1] While David and Solar were

1. David and Solar, 'A Bicentenary Contribution to the History of the Cost of Living in America,' *Research in Economic History*, 2 (1977): 1–80. For Brady, see *ibid.*, 3, and text, n. 14, above.
    Since that article appeared, others have produced complementary data series. See, especially, Winifred B[arr] Rothenberg, 'A Price Index for Rural Massachusetts, 1750–1855,' *Journal of Economic History*, 39 (December 1979): 975–1001. She based her index on farm prices. See also Donald R. Adams, Jr., 'Wage Rates in the Early National Period: Philadelphia, 1785–1830,' *Journal of Economic History*, 28 (September 1968): 404–26; and Adams, 'Prices and Wages in Maryland, 1750–1850,' *Journal of Economic History*, 48 (September 1986): 625–45, a summation of his more extensive treatment of the same subject in 'One Hundred Years of Prices and Wages: Maryland, 1750–1850,' *Working Papers from the Regional Economic History Research Center*, 5 (No. 4, 1985): 90–129. Finally, see Adams, 'Prices and Wages,' in *Encyclopedia of American Economic History: Studies of the Principal Movements and Ideas*, ed. [Patrick] Glenn Porter, 3 vols. (New York: Charles Scribner's Sons, 1980), 1:229–46.
    In addition to the indexes made use of in this book, three others might be mentioned. The two for seventeenth-century Massachusetts are not satisfactory because they are both based on data that are inadequate, inconsistent, and of questionable comparability. See William I. Davisson, 'Essex County Price Trends: Money and Markets in 17th Century Massachusetts,' *Essex Institute Historical Collections*, 103 (April 1967): 141–85; and Terry Lee Anderson, *The Economic Growth of Seventeenth Century New England: A Measurement of Regional Income* ([Ph.D. diss., University of Washington, 1972]; New York: Arno Press, 1975), and Anderson, 'Wealth Estimates for the New England Colonies, 1650–1709,' *Explorations in Economic History*, 12 (April 1975): 151–76. Compare Anderson's comments on Davisson's efforts in Anderson, *Economic Growth of Seventeenth Century New England*, 147–51. Billy G. Smith's index for Philadelphia, 1754–1800, is of limited usefulness because his price data are institutional prices rather than market prices and because the index is purposely biased to exaggerate the impact on the poor because of changes in the cost of a specified 'diet.' It is a case of special pleading. See Smith, '"The Best Poor Man's Country": Living Standards of the "Lower Sort" in Late Eighteenth-Century Philadelphia,' *Working Papers from the Regional Economic History Research Center*, 2 (No. 4, 1979): 1–70; and Smith, *The 'Lower Sort': Philadelphia's Laboring People, 1750–1800* (Ithaca, N.Y.: Cornell University Press, [1990]). Compare the commodity price index for Québec, 1690–1749, by Yvon Desloges, *A Ten-*

aware of some of the earlier studies, they did not pay as much attention to others, most notably the index generated by George Rogers Taylor and Ethel D. Hoover (hereinafter referred to as the Taylor/Hoover index), which stretched back somewhat farther into the colonial era than did David and Solar's.[2] Nevertheless, we can build on what they started.

David and Solar produced a consumer price index, as distinguished from an index of wholesale prices, in order to trace changes in the cost of living over time. In doing so they made the point, noted above, that there was considerable correspondence between the trends of wholesale prices and consumer prices both in their direction and in the timing of changes in direction. Moreover, they found these similarities to have been even greater in the earlier period, a fact that encouraged them, they argue, to project their index back into the colonial period by relying almost exclusively on wholesale prices. 'We have therefore sought to infer the behavior of a consumer price index—which cannot really be constructed by direct means—from the observable movement of wholesale prices.'[3] It is a lesson the implications of which will be applied more broadly in the present discussion.

---

ant's Town: Québec in the 18th Century, [trans. Department of the Secretary of State] ([Ottawa, Ontario: Environment Canada, Parks Service, 1991]), 217–42. As Catherine M. Desbarats, 'Colonial Government Finances in New France, 1700–1750' (Ph.D. diss., McGill University, 1993), 187, n. 52, has observed, the prices that Desloges used are not market prices but prices taken from the inventories of decedents' estates. Compare the series developed by P. M. G. Harris, 'Inflation and Deflation in Early America, 1634–1860: Patterns of Change in the British-American Economy,' *Social Science History*, 20 (Winter 1996): 469–505, which are the basis of the series in Table A-1, Column 1, below. Recalling that such indexes are designed to measure the relative changes of prices over time, just so long as inventory prices retain the same relationship to market prices during that period, they serve their purpose well enough—all other things being equal.

2. [United States, Congress, Joint Economic Committee], *Study of Employment, Growth, and Price Levels: Hearings before the Joint Economic Committee, Congress of the United States . . . April 7, 8, 9, and 10, 1959*, 86th Congress, 2d Session, 10 pts. in 13 vols. (Washington, D.C.: United States Government Printing Office, 1959–1960), Part Two: *Historical and Comparative Rates of Production, Productivity, and Prices*, 379–410. The Taylor/Hoover index is reprinted in [United States, Department of Commerce, Bureau of the Census], *Historical Statistics of the United States, Colonial Times to 1970*, [3d ed.], 2 vols. (Washington, D.C.: United States Government Printing Office, 1975), 2:1196, Series Z 557. Cf. *ibid.*, 1:201, 204–6, Series E 52, 90, 111. See also the index compiled by Jones, *American Colonial Wealth, Documents and Methods*, 3:1719 (Table 3.5). Potential users should beware a problem with a commercial edition of the *Historical Statistics* volume. The 'Correction Sheet' that accompanied the original edition of the work was not included with—nor were the mistakes so noted corrected in—*The Statistical History of the United States, from Colonial Times to the Present*, [ed. Ben J. Wattenberg] (New York: Basic Books, 1976).

3. David and Solar, 'Cost of Living,' 20–21 (quot., p. 21). Compare text, n. 20, above.

Taylor and Hoover compiled a wholesale commodity price index for the period from 1720 to 1958 based on some of the same data that David and Solar used. The Taylor/Hoover index is reproduced as Column 4 in Table A-1. One can grasp immediately the sense of David and Solar's point quoted above: there is an increasing correspondence between the movement of the two indexes the further back in time one looks. This suggests that it is not unreasonable to extend the Brady/David/Solar series even earlier into the eighteenth century. It can be done using the index compiled by Anne Bezanson, which appears in Column 2. The data in the Bezanson index, like those used by David and Solar for the later period and by Taylor and Hoover for the same period, were compiled during the 1930s in a study of commodity prices in the Philadelphia market undertaken by Anne Bezanson and her associates.[4] On the basis of the Bezanson index, the series in Column 6 establishes a composite index that reaches all the way to 1720; the two are spliced at 1774.[5]

The money of account in the United States in the period of the David and Solar index was the United States dollar, the equivalent of the Spanish piece of eight, a silver coin, the *peso de ocho reales*. During the Amer-

4. The Taylor/Hoover index for the colonial era was derived from the separate, earlier studies of prices at Philadelphia, Charleston, and New York, which were originally published independently and later summarized in Arthur Harrison Cole, *Wholesale Commodity Prices in the United States, 1700–1861*, 2 vols. (Cambridge, Massachusetts: Harvard University Press, 1938). For the original studies, see especially Anne Bezanson, Robert D. Gray, and Miriam Hussey, *Prices in Colonial Pennsylvania* (Philadelphia: University of Pennsylvania Press, 1935); Anne Bezanson, Blanch Daley, Marjorie C. Denison and Miriam Hussey, *Prices and Inflation during the American Revolution: Pennsylvania, 1770–1790* (Philadelphia: University of Pennsylvania Press, 1951); and Anne Bezanson, Blanch Daley, Marjorie C. Denison and Miriam Hussey, *Wholesale Prices in Philadelphia, 1784–1861*, 2 vols. (Philadelphia: University of Pennsylvania Press, 1936–37). See also George Rogers Taylor, 'Wholesale Commodity Prices at Charleston, South Carolina, [1732–1861],' *Journal of Economic and Business History*, 4 (February and August 1932): 356–77, 848–[876]; G[eorge] F. Warren, F[rank] A. Pearson, and Herman M. Stoker, *Wholesale Prices for 213 Years, 1720 to 1932*, Cornell University, Agricultural Experiment Station, Memoir 412 (Ithaca, N.Y.: Cornell University, 1932). Compare Rothenberg, 'A Price Index for Rural Massachusetts, 1750–1855'; and Thomas Senior Berry, *Western Prices before 1861: A Study of the Cincinnati Market*, Harvard Economic Studies, Vol. 74 (Cambridge: Harvard University Press, 1943).

5. David and Solar developed a 'markup adjustment model' that they employed for the period 1774–94 to increase, on average, by 8.87%, the wholesale commodity price index, the better to approximate, in their view, the consumer price index (David and Solar, 'Cost of Living,' 52–55). That adjustment is ignored herein if only because such a difference is wholly inadequate as an expression of the usual 'advance,' or markup, from wholesale to retail prices, thus calling into question the entire exercise. It is more important to realize the close association of wholesale and retail prices and their consequent movement in parallel. Compare text, n. 20, above.

ican Revolutionary War, paper currency depreciated in worth against the silver dollar (see Appendix C). David and Solar took this into account for the years 1774 to 1784 by adjusting their index by 'an annual series of specie price relatives.'[6] It was necessary to do so in order to express all of their prices in the same currency, the hard dollar.

A similar adjustment is necessary to extend the series to an even earlier period. In the years before the American Revolutionary War, the money of account at Philadelphia was Pennsylvania pounds currency. An annual series of specie price relatives for the years from 1720 to 1774 was constructed on the basis of the exchange rate between Pennsylvania currency and pounds sterling. At par, £166.67 Pennsylvania currency equalled £100 sterling. As John Wright, author of *The American Negotiator: or The Various Currencies of the British Colonies in America*, wrote in 1767: 'the exact equitable Pars of Exchange in any of the Provinces is, the nominal Value of the Spanish milled Dollar or Ounce of Silver. . . .'[7] The dollar or piece of eight was worth, at par, 4s 6d sterling (22.5p) and 7s 6d Pennsylvania currency; £1 sterling was equivalent, at par, to $4.44. The relationship of Pennsylvania pounds currency to specie varied directly as Pennsylvania currency varied against the pound sterling. The Bezanson index series was adjusted by the reciprocal of the index of the Pennsylvania-to-sterling exchange rate index to convert it to a dollar basis.[8] While the figures in Column 6 for the years from 1720 to 1773 are clearly less satisfactory as a commodity price index than are those for later years, there are reasons nevertheless for thinking it not wholly unacceptable.[9]

It is additionally possible to extend the composite index in Column 6 even further backward and forward in time. Newly available data for the United States now reaches to the mid-seventeenth century. (The numbers for Britain are already of significant lineage; they are taken from a

6. David and Solar, 'Cost of Living,' 49.

7. Wright, *The American Negotiator: or The Various Currencies of the British Colonies in America; As Well the Islands, as the Continent. . . . Reduced into English Money . . .* , 3rd ed. (London: The Author, 1767), lxiv. For the par value of the dollar and the pound sterling, see also Appendix C, n. 18, below.

8. For a full explanation of this process, see Stephen G. Hardy, 'Trade and Economic Growth in the Eighteenth-Century Chesapeake' (Ph.D. diss., University of Maryland, 1999), 339–421.

9. The overall correlation of all such indexes is the most compelling of such reasons (see this appendix, n. 18, below). Another reason is the crude but nevertheless comforting correlation between the United States commodity price index and that for Britain. See Appendix D below, and the chart in Figure 1, p. 30.

series that begins with 1264.) This new research is an outgrowth of the investigations by scholars over the last three decades into the economy of the colonial Chesapeake region, investigations begun by and subsequently pursued under the direction of Lois G. Carr. Based on the commodity valuations that contemporaries employed in the inventorying of decedents' estates, one of the people associated with the project, P. M. G. Harris, has developed indexes of those prices for Maryland and Virginia ranging from the 1630s into the nineteenth century.[10]

A second scholar, Stephen G. Hardy, has recently taken a critical look at the Harris data and made a set of significant adjustments to overcome some problems found with them for present purposes.[11] Most importantly, the prices upon which Harris based his calculations were, like Bezanson's prices, expressed in colonial currency, in this instance in the different currencies of the two colonies, Maryland and Virginia. Employing the admittedly fragmentary exchange rate data for these two colonies, Hardy has converted each of the two Harris indexes to dollar figures in order to calculate an average index number for them and then to link that average to other index numbers based on dollars, specifically the Bezanson and the David and Solar indexes in Table A-1. The Harris series, modified by Hardy, fluctuated after 1720 in tandem with indexes based on market prices, and this suggests that we can rely on the Harris/Hardy index for at least some indication of the way commodity prices fluctuated for the entire period from 1665 through 1720.[12] Splicing occurs in the latter year. The linkage of the Harris/Hardy numbers with the others in Table A-1 results in an index—even if a less-than-perfect one—that extends from the earliest years of the colonial period to our own time.[13]

10. Harris, 'Inflation and Deflation in Early America, 1634–1860: Patterns of Change in the British-American Economy,' *Social Science History*, 20 (Winter 1996): 469–505. Harris has most generously authorized me to reproduce his data. I continue to be very grateful for his help.

11. Hardy, 'Trade and Economic Growth in the Eighteenth-Century Chesapeake,' 339–421.

12. For the first edition of this study, a commodity price index for the period from 1700 to 1719 was constructed using prices for six commodities from Philadelphia. It has been discarded in lieu of the better Chesapeake data from Harris as modified by Hardy.

13. Harris presents data for the years before 1665 that are not incorporated into the series in Table A-1. They are thought to be less satisfactory than those for the later period. Notwithstanding, it is possible to estimate the colonial commodity price index for years prior to 1666 by using the ratio between the British commodity price index and the colo-

Utilizing many of these same procedures, the Brady/David/Solar index in Table A-1, Column 3, can be brought forward from 1974 into the 1990s and beyond. We accomplish this by basing our calculations on the consumer price index compiled and published monthly and annually by the United States Bureau of Labor Statistics (see Table A-1, Column 5, as discussed above). That, indeed, is the index that David and Solar used for the years 1914–74; here it is merely extended forward another quarter century.[14] The reader can carry on this process by taking the monthly and annual index numbers when they are released by the Bureau of Labor Statistics and splicing them into the series presented here.[15]

Linking these several series is critical to constructing the long-term index necessary for extended comparisons. The process of splicing the

_____

nial commodity price index from later periods. For instance, one can estimate a value for the colonial commodity price index for 1650 by calculating the ratio between the two indexes for the years 1665–1675 (2.35 to 1) and then presuming that same ratio applied earlier (Table A-1, Column 6; Table D-1, Column 4). Given an average British commodity price index for 1648–52 of 57.6, the resulting estimated colonial commodity price index for the five-year period centered on 1650 is 135. See the discussion in Appendix D, below.

14. We use the CPI-U, the more broadly structured 'Consumer Price Index for all Urban Consumers (CPI-U),' on a reference base of 1982–1984 = 100. In February 1978 the Division of Consumer Prices and Price Indexes, Bureau of Labor Statistics (BLS) began compiling and releasing two index numbers, the result of a long-term project to revise the whole procedure of data collection and compilation. See [United States, Department of Labor, Bureau of Labor Statistics], *The Consumer Price Index: Concepts and Content over the Years*, Bureau of Labor Statistics, Report 517, rev. ed. (Washington, D.C.: United States Government Printing Office, 1978); *BLS Handbook of Methods*, 154–215.

15. The BLS announces the index number for any given month about the middle of the next month; the same office announces the index number for the year about the middle of January. It operates a 'CPI Quickline' (1-202-606-6994) that plays a recorded message reporting and commenting on the monthly numbers. The address of the BLS website is http://stats.bls.gov. Monthly releases of the price index data are accessible at http://stats.bls.gov.

The BLS data series are republished in a number of places. Probably the easiest access to the most recent figures can be had in the tables distributed every month as the 'Summary of CPI News Release.' The BLS *Monthly Labor Review* contains both the data and analyses of short-term and long-term price trends. The data are published in late January or early February in the presidential report on the state of the economy. In the [United States, President], *Economic Report of the President . . . 2000* (Washington, D.C.: United States Government Printing Office, 2000), 376, Table B-60 shows the BLS consumer price index annually for the years 1958 to 1999, as well as monthly for 1998 and 1999. One can also consult the current [United States, Department of Commerce, Bureau of the Census], *Statistical Abstract of the United States* (Washington, D.C.: United States Government Printing Office). Various additional series and a most useful introduction to the whole subject are available as part of the *Historical Statistics of the United States*, 1:183–214 (see esp. 183–84).

Harris/Hardy series with the Bezanson index and the Bureau of Labor Statistics post-1974 index into the Brady/David/Solar index is necessary because, as originally computed, each had a different reference base period. For all the indexes to be comparable, we must convert them to the same reference base.[16] The base year of the Brady/David/Solar series is 1860 = 100; the Taylor/Hoover index has the period 1850–59 = 100 as its base; the Bezanson index, 1774; the Harris/Hardy index, although tied to the index reported here, used as a base 1700–29 = 100; the Bureau of Labor Statistics series uses 1982–84 = 100.

Splicing reduces the Bureau of Labor Statistics, the Bezanson, the Taylor/Hoover and the Harris/Hardy indexes to a new reference base year, 1860 = 100. These linkages are realized in Table A-1, Column 6. All that has to be done to accomplish the linkages is to vary the annual number for Column 6 by the same percentage that it changes in each of the other columns, as appropriate. For instance, according to the Bureau of Labor Statistics series (Column 5), the increase in the consumer price index in 1978 over 1977 was 7.6% (65.2 ÷ 60.6 = 1.076). On base 1860 = 100, the composite commodity price index number for 1977 is 725 (Column 6); an increase of 7.6% means that for 1978 the number 780 (725 x 1.076 = 780). Should anyone wish to employ a different reference base, a simple variation on this method will accomplish this. Merely divide each annual number by the number for the year or years of the new reference base period.[17]

The extension of the data in Table A-1, Column 6, from 1665 to the present permits us to compare sums in real terms with those from any later time over almost the entire history of the United States.[18]

---

16. For a discussion of the subject, with examples, see Hoover, 'Index Numbers: Practical Applications,' *International Encyclopedia of the Social Sciences*, ed. Sills, 7:161.

17. See the thoughtful discussion of the issues in Roderick Floud, *An Introduction to Quantitative Methods for Historians*, 2nd ed. (London: Methuen, [1979]), 122–29.

18. The use of an index constructed using prices at New York or Philadelphia in the eighteenth and nineteenth centuries—and, earlier, from the Chesapeake Bay region—to derive a commodity price index for the whole of the United States is justified in both fact and theory. Intercolonial trade, even more powerfully when more limited colonial economies were linked by waterborne commerce than later when states were connected by road, canal and railroad, served to facilitate commercial arbitrage and thereby to maintain a certain commonality in the pricing of goods, even over the short haul. Not only would we expect this to be the case, but it proves to have been so upon investigation. Reductions in the costs of information and transportation go far to explain the increasing integration of markets and the diminution in the difference of prices across such markets. Compare the conclusions drawn from the several studies conducted under the aegis of the Interna-

————

tional Scientific Committee on Price History as summarized by Cole, *Wholesale Commodity Prices in the United States*, 1:94–114 (quot., pp. 95–96): '. . . all the results . . . indicate increasing agreement among such movements [of the general price indices] . . . as the
decades pass.' This is even more obvious when we reduce prices to their equivalence in
sterling; prices in the various ports can be seen to have moved in parallel. For the separate
studies that Cole summarized and to which he referred, see this appendix, n. 4, above. The
scholar who has studied these phenomena most recently and most intensively, Winifred B.
Rothenberg, has argued the point most powerfully when she observed 'how strikingly the
cyclical movements of Massachusetts farm produce prices mirrors the cyclical movement
of general wholesale prices in the big-city markets of New York and Philadelphia.' Rothenberg, 'A Price Index for Rural Massachusetts, 1750–1885,' 980. Such synchronicity was
hardly a statistical accident because, as she argues, the coastwise markets of the United
States were increasingly tightly integrated. These themes, developed in her articles, were
repeated and elaborated in her book, *From Market-Places to a Market Economy: The Transformation of Rural Massachusetts, 1750–1850* (Chicago, Illinois: University of Chicago Press,
1992). The growing synchronicity and congruence, even convergence among markets, the
last stages of which Rothenberg chronicles, had their beginnings very early in the seventeenth century, as soon as businessmen learned that there were sellers and buyers up and
down the North American coast for nearly everything they had to buy and sell. See, e.g.,
the comment by Governor John Harvey that 'Virginia is become (like another Sicily to
home) the Granary of all his Majesties northerne Collonies.' Letter from Harvey, at Virginia, to [Secretary of State Francis Windebank], at London, July 14, 1634, Colonial Office
Records, CO 1/8, fol. 74r, Public Record Office, London. For the development of the
coastwise trade in the 18th century, see David C. Klingaman, *Colonial Virginia's Coastwise
and Grain Trade* ([Ph.D. diss., University of Virginia, 1967]; New York: Arno Press, 1989).

TABLE A-1

COMMODITY PRICE INDEXES, UNITED STATES, 1665–2000

Year (Base =)	Harris/ Hardy (1720–29)	Bezanson (1774)	Brady/ David/ Solar (1860)	Taylor/ Hoover (1859–60)	Bureau of Labor Statistics (1982–84)	Composite Commodity Price Index (1860)
	1	2	3	4	5	6
1665	131					106
1666	132					106
1667	142					114
1668	147					118
1669	137					110
1670	134					108
1671	138					110
1672	136					109
1673	130					104
1674	139					112
1675	121					97
1676	122					98
1677	123					99
1678	120					97
1679	120					96
1680	137					110
1681	141					113
1682	115					92
1683	114					92
1684	115					92
1685	123					99
1686	116					93
1687	116					93
1688	106					85
1689	109					87
1690	110					89
1691	116					93

Year (Base =)	Harris/ Hardy (1720–29)	Bezanson (1774)	Brady/ David/ Solar (1860)	Taylor/ Hoover (1859–60)	Bureau of Labor Statistics (1982–84)	Composite Commodity Price Index (1860)
	1	2	3	4	5	6
1692	110					88
1693	103					83
1694	110					88
1695	101					81
1696	119					95
1697	116					93
1698	110					88
1699	120					96
1700	116					93
1701	122					98
1702	113					90
1703	111					89
1704	126					101
1705	114					91
1706	122					98
1707	118					94
1708	93					74
1709	111					89
1710	100					80
1711	98					79
1712	93					75
1713	99					80
1714	91					73
1715	102					82
1716	96					77
1717	103					82
1718	97					77
1719	102					82
1720	94	78		59		76
1721	109	73		53		71

Year (Base =)	Harris/ Hardy (1720–29)	Bezanson (1774)	Brady/ David/ Solar (1860)	Taylor/ Hoover (1859–60)	Bureau of Labor Statistics (1982–84)	Composite Commodity Price Index (1860)
	1	2	3	4	5	6
1722	107	77		56		75
1723	99	78		57		76
1724	107	82		60		79
1725	100	93		66		90
1726	93	85		69		83
1727	91	89		66		86
1728	96	83		63		81
1729	104	82		63		80
1730		83		67		80
1731		73		59		71
1732		69		58		66
1733		70		60		68
1734		68		67		66
1735		70		66		68
1736		67		63		65
1737		69		69		67
1738		72		69		70
1739		64		60		62
1740		68		60		66
1741		94		74		91
1742		84		70		81
1743		73		60		71
1744		69		57		66
1745		66		54		64
1746		67		55		65
1747		74		66		72
1748		85		74		82
1749		87		76		84
1750		87		74		84
1751		88		72		85

Year (Base =)	Harris/ Hardy (1720–29)	Bezanson (1774)	Brady/ David/ Solar (1860)	Taylor/ Hoover (1859–60)	Bureau of Labor Statistics (1982–84)	Composite Commodity Price Index (1860)
	1	2	3	4	5	6
1752		89		76		86
1753		87		78		84
1754		84		71		81
1755		81		71		79
1756		80		70		77
1757		84		70		81
1758		89		74		87
1759		102		86		99
1760		99		82		96
1761		90		78		88
1762		98		83		95
1763		98		84		95
1764		90		77		88
1765		92		77		89
1766		100		82		97
1767		98		82		95
1768		93		81		90
1769		95		81		93
1770		103		80		100
1771		99		85		96
1772		113		98		110
1773		105		91		102
1774		100	97	84		97
1775			92	78		92
1776			105	108		105
1777			128	330		128
1778			166	598		166
1779			147	2,969		147
1780			165	10,544		165
1781			133	5,086		133
1782			146	140		146

Year (Base =)	Harris/ Hardy (1720–29)	Bezanson (1774)	Brady/ David/ Solar (1860)	Taylor/ Hoover (1859–60)	Bureau of Labor Statistics (1982–84)	Composite Commodity Price Index (1860)
	1	2	3	4	5	6
1783			128	119		128
1784			123	113		123
1785			117	105		117
1786			114	105		114
1787			112	104		112
1788			107	97		107
1789			106	94		106
1790			110	100		110
1791			113	98		113
1792			115	101		115
1793			119	109		119
1794			132	122		132
1795			151	146		151
1796			159	158		159
1797			153	143		153
1798			148	139		148
1799			148	142		148
1800			151	141		151
1801			153	151		153
1802			129	129		129
1803			136	128		136
1804			142	136		142
1805			141	148		141
1806			147	140		147
1807			139	135		139
1808			151	122		151
1809			148	134		148
1810			148	137		148
1811			158	133		158
1812			160	137		160
1813			192	161		192

Year (Base =)	Harris/ Hardy (1720–29)	Bezanson (1774)	Brady/ David/ Solar (1860)	Taylor/ Hoover (1859–60)	Bureau of Labor Statistics (1982–84)	Composite Commodity Price Index (1860)
	1	2	3	4	5	6
1814			211	184		211
1815			185	183		185
1816			169	177		169
1817			160	173		160
1818			153	169		153
1819			153	141		153
1820			141	117		141
1821			136	107		136
1822			141	113		141
1823			126	105		126
1824			116	102		116
1825			119	112		119
1826			119	100		119
1827			120	97		120
1828			114	96		114
1829			112	95		112
1830			111	91		111
1831			104	92		104
1832			103	95		103
1833			101	98		101
1834			103	95		103
1835			106	109		106
1836			112	122		112
1837			115	114		115
1838			112	110		112
1839			112	115		112
1840			104	95		104
1841			105	93		105
1842			98	81		98
1843			89	75		89
1844			90	78		90

Year (Base =)	Harris/ Hardy (1720–29)	Bezanson (1774)	Brady/ David/ Solar (1860)	Taylor/ Hoover (1859–60)	Bureau of Labor Statistics (1982–84)	Composite Commodity Price Index (1860)
	1	2	3	4	5	6
1845			91	82		91
1846			92	83		92
1847			99	93		99
1848			95	78		95
1849			92	82		92
1850			94	91		94
1851			92	87		92
1852			93	88		93
1853			93	96		93
1854			101	103		101
1855			104	110		104
1856			102	110		102
1857			105	119		105
1858			99	98		99
1859			100	101		100
1860			100	100		100
1861			106	103		106
1862			121	120		121
1863			151	152		151
1864			189	221		189
1865			196	211		196
1866			191	197		191
1867			178	183		178
1868			171	177		171
1869			164	168		164
1870			157	149		157
1871			147	143		147
1872			147	152		147
1873			144	146		144
1874			137	138		137
1875			132	131		132

Year (Base =)	Harris/ Hardy (1720–29)	Bezanson (1774)	Brady/ David/ Solar (1860)	Taylor/ Hoover (1859–60)	Bureau of Labor Statistics (1982–84)	Composite Commodity Price Index (1860)
	1	2	3	4	5	6
1876			129	120		129
1877			126	117		126
1878			120	100		120
1879			120	98		120
1880			123	110		123
1881			123	112		123
1882			123	116		123
1883			121	108		121
1884			118	100		118
1885			116	92		116
1886			113	89		113
1887			114	92		114
1888			114	94		114
1889			111	90		111
1890			109	91		109
1891			109	90		109
1892			109	84		109
1893			108	86		108
1894			103	77		103
1895			101	79		101
1896			101	75		101
1897			100	75		100
1898			100	78		100
1899			100	84		100
1900			101	91		101
1901			102	89		102
1902			103	95		103
1903			106	96		106
1904			107	96		107
1905			106	97		106
1906			108	100		108

Year (Base =)	Harris/ Hardy (1720–29)	Bezanson (1774)	Brady/ David/ Solar (1860)	Taylor/ Hoover (1859–60)	Bureau of Labor Statistics (1982–84)	Composite Commodity Price Index (1860)
	1	2	3	4	5	6
1907			113	105		113
1908			111	102		111
1909			109	109		109
1910			114	114		114
1911			114	105		114
1912			117	112		117
1913			119	113		119
1914			120	110		120
1915			121	112		121
1916			130	138		130
1917			153	190		153
1918			180	212		180
1919			207	224		207
1920			240	249		240
1921			214	158		214
1922			200	156		200
1923			204	163		204
1924			204	158		204
1925			210	167		210
1926			211	162		211
1927			208	154		208
1928			205	156		205
1929			205	154		205
1930			200	140		200
1931			182	118		182
1932			163	105		163
1933			155	106		155
1934			160	121		160
1935			164	129		164
1936			166	131		166
1937			172	139		172

Year (Base =)	Harris/ Hardy (1720–29)	Bezanson (1774)	Brady/ David/ Solar (1860)	Taylor/ Hoover (1859–60)	Bureau of Labor Statistics (1982–84)	Composite Commodity Price Index (1860)
	1	2	3	4	5	6
1938			169	127		169
1939			166	125		166
1940			168	127		168
1941			176	141		176
1942			195	160		195
1943			207	167		207
1944			210	168		210
1945			215	171		215
1946			233	196		233
1947			267	240		267
1948			288	259		288
1949			285	247		285
1950			288	256		288
1951			310	285		310
1952			317	277		317
1953			320	274		320
1954			321	274		321
1955			320	275		320
1956			325	284		325
1957			336	292		336
1958			346	296		346
1959			348			348
1960			354			354
1961			358			358
1962			362			362
1963			366			366
1964			371			371
1965			377			377
1966			388			388
1967			399			399
1968			416			416
1969			438			438

Year (Base =)	Harris/ Hardy (1720–29)	Bezanson (1774)	Brady/ David/ Solar (1860)	Taylor/ Hoover (1859–60)	Bureau of Labor Statistics (1982–84)	Composite Commodity Price Index (1860)
	1	2	3	4	5	6
1970			464		39	464
1971			484		41	484
1972			500		42	500
1973			531		44	531
1974			589		49	590
1975					54	643
1976					57	680
1977					61	725
1978					65	780
1979					73	868
1980					82	985
1981					91	1,087
1982					97	1,154
1983					100	1,191
1984					104	1,243
1985					108	1,287
1986					110	1,311
1987					114	1,359
1988					118	1,415
1989					124	1,483
1990					131	1,563
1991					136	1,629
1992					140	1,678
1993					144	1,728
1994					148	1,773
1995					152	1,822
1996					157	1,876
1997					161	1,920
1998					163	1,949
1999					167	1,992
2000					172	2,059

Year (Base =)	Harris/ Hardy (1720–29)	Bezanson (1774)	Brady/ David/ Solar (1860)	Taylor/ Hoover (1859–60)	Bureau of Labor Statistics (1982–84)	Composite Commodity Price Index (1860)
	1	2	3	4	5	6
2001						2,111 (est.)
2002						
2003						
2004						
2005						
2006						
2007						
2008						
2009						

NOTES AND SOURCES: The dates in the column headings are the reference base periods (e.g., 1720–1729 = 100). The figures in Column 1 are from P. M. G. Harris, 'Inflation and Deflation in Early America, 1634–1860: Patterns of Change in the British-American Economy,' *Social Science History*, 20 (Winter 1996): 469–505, as recalculated by Stephen G. Hardy, 'Trade and Economic Growth in the Eighteenth-Century Chesapeake' (Ph.D. diss., University of Maryland, 1999), 405–9 (Table 33, first column: 'Chesapeake Average Specie Index'), as discussed in the text, above. The figures in Column 2 are from Anne Bezanson, Robert D. Gray, and Miriam Hussey, *Prices in Colonial Pennsylvania* (Philadelphia: University of Pennsylvania Press, 1935), 433 (twenty commodities, arithmetic index), modified and restated as a dollar-based series as discussed in the text, above. Column 3 is from Table 1 in Paul A. David and Peter Solar, 'A Bicentenary Contribution to the History of the Cost of Living in America,' *Research in Economic History* (1977) 2:16–17. Column 4 is from [United States, Congress, Joint Economic Committee], *Study of Employment, Growth, and Price Levels: Hearings before the Joint Economic Committee, Congress of the United States . . . April 7, 8, 9, and 10, 1959*, 86th Congress, 2d Session, 10 parts in 13 vols. (Washington, D.C.: United States Government Printing Office, 1959–60), Part Two: *Historical and Comparative Rates of Production, Productivity, and Prices*, 394–97. Column 5 is from the monthly and annual releases by the Bureau of Labor Statistics, for the details of which see the discussion above. Especially useful are the monthly press releases issued by the Bureau of Labor Statistics at its website: http://stats.bls.gov. Column 6 links Column 1, Column 2, and Column 5 with Column 3 and converts the three of them to the Column 5 reference base period (1860 = 100) as described in the text, above. Linkage or splicing is at 1720, 1774 and 1971. The estimate for the year 2001 is based on the Federal Reserve Bank of Philadelphia/Survey of Professional Forecasters' expectation that the rate of inflation over the decade 2000–2009 will average 2.5%. For this estimate, see their quarterly survey reports at: http://www.phil.frb.org. For an evaluation of this and other estimates, see Lloyd B. Thomas, Jr., 'Survey Measures of Expected U.S. Inflation,' *Journal of Economic Perspectives* 13 (Fall 1999): 125–44.

APPENDIX B

RATES OF EXCHANGE —
THE RELATIONSHIPS OF THE CURRENCIES OF
THE CONTINENTAL COLONIES TO GREAT
BRITAIN AND TO EACH OTHER, 1649–1775

Each of the continental colonies, separate politically as well as economically, maintained its own currency.[1] The money of account employed by Massachusetts and that employed by New York, even if both were called 'pounds,' were just as different from each other as the dollars of Canada, the United States, Jamaica, and Hong Kong are in our own day. Moreover, for accounting purposes, some of these differences were maintained into the nineteenth century, well after the official adoption in 1785 of the United States dollar as the new national currency, the new real money.[2]

There are two implications of these differences for users of this book. The first is obvious and easily inferred from what has just been said. In order to compare two values expressed in the currencies of two separate colonies, they must be reduced to a common denominator. Faced with this problem, people in the seventeenth and eighteenth centuries had three choices. They could reduce both sums to pounds sterling, the money of account of the Mother Country. If they preferred, they could convert the sum expressed in the currency of one colony into that of the second colony. Colonists found this somewhat cumbersome to accomplish because rarely was there systematic information available about intercolonial exchange rates. The rates of exchange between the colonies and London were far better known and publicized than were intercolonial rates simply because a market for the former existed and a market for the latter did not.[3] The third option open to colonists was to express the sum in question in terms of the dollar, the Spanish *peso de ocho reales*, or the piece of eight.[4]

1. Compare the empires of the other European nations and their colonies, all of which is treated in some detail in McCusker, *Money and Exchange in Europe and America, 1600–1775*.
2. See the discussion in Appendix C, below.
3. See McCusker, *Money and Exchange in Europe and America*, passim.
4. For the *peso de ocho reales*, see Appendix C, below.

It was fairly convenient to reduce sums in colonial moneys of account into dollars because everyone knew just how much their local pounds were worth in dollars. Their pounds were a money of account. Dollars were their real money. Until the advent of paper money—and afterwards, too—the coins in peoples' pockets and purses were dollars—pieces of eight—and the smaller sub-units of the dollar, the 'bits.'[5] A commodity priced in the marketplace at so many shillings and pence was paid for with dollars and parts of a dollar, a half-dollar or a quarter-dollar. So pervasive was the peso that colonial governments passed laws fixing the worth of their pounds currency in terms of the dollar, thereby setting the par of exchange.[6] To settle a debt across colonial borders, the simplest thing to do was to express it in terms of dollars and to pay it with dollars.

The second implication of these differences for readers is directly related to the first: they need to know the rates of exchange between colonial currencies in order to make use of the tables in this book if their comparisons involve colonial currency. Table A-1 is expressed in dollars. Table 1 shows the necessity of reducing a sum in pounds currency to its contemporary dollar equivalent before determining the ratio necessary to compare it with some later or earlier time. In both instances, the sum in colonial money of account is first converted to pounds sterling and then into dollars at the set rate for the era. (That both the pound sterling and the Spanish dollar remained extraordinarily stable over the centuries makes such a process possible for such a long period.[7]) Thus it is essential that we know the rate of exchange between colonial currencies and sterling.

That is the point of this Appendix. Table B-1 shows the rates of exchange on an annual average basis between the currencies of nine of the

5. There was a variety of other coinage in circulation, of course—Spanish silver and gold, Portuguese gold, Dutch silver (and some gold)—but the piece of eight dominated the world's, and the colonists', coinage. McCusker, *Money and Exchange in Europe and America*, 7. Compare Oscar G. Schilke and Raphael E. Solomon, *America's Foreign Coins: An Illustrated Standard Catalogue with Valuations of Foreign Coins with Legal Tender Status in the United States, 1793–1857* (New York: Coin and Currency Institute, 1964); and Solomon, 'Foreign Specie Coins in the American Colonies,' in *Studies on Money in Early America*, ed. Eric P. Newman and Richard G. Doty (New York: American Numismatic Society, 1976), 25–42. See also David A. Martin, 'The Changing Role of Foreign Money in the United States, 1782–1857,' *Journal of Economic History*, 37 (December 1977): 1009–27.

6. See again, Appendix C, below.

7. McCusker, *Money and Exchange in Europe and America*, 7–8. Compare, yet again, Appendix C, below, esp. n. 13.

Continental Colonies and sterling from as early as we have data through 1775. Massachusetts so dominated New England that its currency exchange rate applied as well in New Hampshire, Rhode Island, and Connecticut; Delaware was closely dependant on Pennsylvania for its currency, as for much else. There are exceptions to both statements. Nevertheless, the table covers all of the Continental Colonies, for practical purposes.[8]

8. I cannot let the opportunity pass without saying that these data are the result of a nearly forty-year-long effort to collect and compile exchange rates and, as all will notice, there are still serious gaps in many series. Anyone who would care to share data with me to help fill those gaps will find a warm welcome. I need a full citation to the source of any such data and, ideally, a photocopy of the document.

The rate of exchange on London in the british continental colonies, 1649–1775

Year	Massachusetts	New York	New Jersey	Pennsylvania	Maryland (Hard Currency)	Maryland (Paper Currency)	Virginia	North Carolina	South Carolina	Georgia
1649	112.00									
1650										
1651										
1652										
1653										
1654										
1655										
1656										
1657										
1658										
1659										
1660	112.00									
1661	112.00									
1662	112.00									
1663	112.00									
1664	113.33									
1665	115.33									

1666	115.67		
1667	116.00		
1668	115.75		
1669	116.00		
1670	125.00		
1671	125.00		
1672	125.00		
1673	125.00		
1674	125.00		
1675	123.89		
1676	129.17		
1677	128.00		
1678	128.00		
1679	122.00		
1680	120.25	125.00	
1681	124.88		
1682	128.00		
1683	128.00		125.00
1684	130.00		125.00
1685	127.50		126.00
1686	125.00		127.00

Year	Massachusetts	New York	New Jersey	Pennsylvania	Maryland (Hard Currency)	Maryland (Paper Currency)	Virginia	North Carolina	South Carolina	Georgia
1687	120.94			128.00						
1688	140.00	130.06		129.00						
1689	134.17			130.00						
1690	128.33			131.17			110.00			
1691	131.25			132.34						
1692	130.50			133.52						
1693	130.00			134.69						
1694	133.66	129.16		135.86						
1695	139.86	130.00		142.93						
1696	129.17	130.00		150.00						
1697	136.00	130.00		150.00						
1698	138.24	130.00		150.00						
1699	140.48	132.48		149.31						
1700	139.43	134.96		148.61						
1701	136.50	132.50		147.92						
1702	130.00	133.33		150.70	111.11					
1703	140.00	140.00	166.67	150.84					150.00	
1704	140.00			150.00					150.00	
1705	135.00			150.14					150.00	

Year								
1706	150.00			150.21		115.00		150.00
1707	150.35			152.92		112.54		150.00
1708	150.71			153.65		110.08		150.00
1709	151.06	150.00		133.07		107.62		150.00
1710	155.00	145.05		127.99		108.06		150.00
1711	146.67	151.12		128.99		108.50		150.00
1712	150.00	155.62		129.98		110.00		150.00
1713	150.00	153.75		131.68		110.00		150.00
1714	153.33	154.90		131.85		110.00		200.00
1715	160.33	153.20		130.16		108.50		300.00
1716	162.50	157.78	142.86	133.68		107.00	150.00	300.00
1717	170.00	160.00	146.97	134.83		105.50		443.75
1718	200.00	157.09	151.07	132.22		108.00		562.50
1719	216.68	154.17	155.18	135.42	113.33	110.50		468.00
1720	219.43	162.92	155.37	138.75	133.33	115.00		536.88
1721	225.98	163.33	155.55	137.50	114.36	115.00		553.44
1722	229.79	164.28		134.98	127.50	115.00	500.00	547.86
1723	241.81	165.22		140.38	128.78	115.00	500.00	650.00
1724	267.92	165.00		144.43	128.39	116.44	500.00	675.00
1725	289.11	165.00		146.33	128.00	117.50		670.49
1726	290.98	165.00		160.00	130.75	114.34		700.00

Year	Massachusetts	New York	New Jersey	Pennsylvania	Maryland (Hard Currency)	Maryland (Paper Currency)	Virginia	North Carolina	South Carolina	Georgia
1727	291.98	165.00		149.59	133.50		116.29		700.00	
1728	298.82	165.00		150.63	136.25		120.00		700.00	
1729	313.33	165.00		149.03	133.33		118.75	500.00	700.00	
1730	337.71	166.88		152.03	133.33		119.92	575.00	693.75	
1731	334.31	165.00		153.42	133.37		122.33	650.00	700.00	
1732	339.51	165.00		161.68	133.33		121.16	675.00	700.00	
1733	350.00	165.00		163.75	133.33	120.00	120.58	700.00	700.00	
1734	355.00	165.00		171.67	133.33	160.00	120.00	710.00	700.00	
1735	360.00	165.00		166.11	133.33	140.00	120.00	720.00	755.00	
1736	430.00	165.00		165.44	133.42	230.00	122.70	700.00	740.73	
1737	516.67	165.00	170.00	169.42	140.00	250.00	121.63	866.67	752.90	
1738	500.00	165.00	169.17	163.13	135.42	225.00	123.75	933.34	785.00	
1739	500.00	166.67	168.33	170.00	137.30	212.34	122.50	1,000.00	788.68	
1740	525.00	166.25	160.62	165.56	139.17	228.08	119.17	966.66	796.67	
1741	548.44	159.44	142.50	146.47	138.82	238.17	120.53	1,000.00	709.08	
1742	550.28	170.97	150.00	159.38	138.64	275.00	120.00		698.96	
1743	550.70	174.67	160.00	160.42	137.78	285.13	120.00		700.00	
1744	588.61	175.42	167.50	165.83	139.44	166.67	121.88		700.00	
1745	644.79	183.33	175.00	172.45	140.00	200.00	127.60	1,000.00	700.00	

Year										
1746	642.50	185.83	182.50	179.77	137.78	210.00	131.87	1,000.00	750.00	108.50
1747	925.00	191.46	178.33	182.80	142.50	225.22	135.01	1,016.67	761.02	
1748	912.50	183.39	174.17	174.07	140.97	200.61	132.29	1,033.33	768.75	
1749	1,033.33	176.46	170.00	171.28	136.32	184.58	123.75		724.67	
1750	137.33	179.33	173.75	170.65	131.66	177.92	125.94	133.33	702.35	
1751	133.33	181.50	172.50	169.86	140.00	166.83	128.42		700.00	
1752	131.67	175.92	166.25	167.48	145.00	155.62	129.92		700.00	
1753	130.00	179.39	167.50	167.48	150.00	151.75	129.50		700.00	
1754	133.33	179.72	168.17	168.25	159.58	153.75	127.55	166.67	700.00	
1755	133.33	180.13	170.00	168.90	165.00	161.88	129.38	160.00	700.00	
1756	133.33	182.65	165.92	172.58	165.00	170.00	128.44	179.80	708.87	
1757	133.33	178.40	166.10	165.80	164.53	145.00	139.71	181.53	700.28	
1758	128.34	172.60	161.25	158.99	157.01	150.00	137.92	183.27	700.00	
1759	128.94	168.39	156.25	153.55	153.75	150.00	139.97	185.00	700.00	
1760	129.54	167.20	153.30	159.44	154.58	146.25	141.43	190.00	700.00	
1761	140.10	181.41	171.25	173.39	168.58	148.48	143.72	200.00	700.00	
1762	142.33	189.76	176.88	176.05	170.65	144.45	152.40	200.00	700.00	
1763	136.00	186.73	169.83	172.97	167.24	140.00	159.88	200.00	716.61	
1764	133.75	184.85	172.02	172.84	166.77	136.66	160.73	192.67	717.80	
1765	133.54	182.80	166.01	170.30	166.65	133.33	160.36	200.00	710.50	
1766	133.03	177.18	160.00	163.55	163.99		128.48	186.48	702.33	

Year	Massachusetts	New York	New Jersey	Pennsylvania	Maryland (Hard Currency)	Maryland (Paper Currency)	Virginia	North Carolina	South Carolina	Georgia
1767	133.33	178.96		165.97	164.59		125.54	172.96	700.00	
1768	133.33	179.87		166.60	164.92		124.99	180.00	699.91	108.93
1769	129.86	172.47		157.69	160.68		121.97		700.39	
1770	126.31	165.90		153.90	151.03		118.00		692.76	
1771	133.33	178.43		165.66	161.84		123.60		694.46	
1772	131.00	173.27		160.61	158.63		123.59	160.00	681.96	108.76
1773	132.19	177.71		166.46	165.13		129.75	167.50	711.84	
1774	135.30	180.62	169.50	169.66	167.10		130.30	175.00	725.56	
1775	117.45	171.55		161.28	156.68		120.00		734.44	108.00

NOTES AND SOURCES: The data in these tables are from John J. McCusker, *Money and Exchange in Europe and America, 1600–1775: A Handbook*, (2d ed., 1992), 315–17 (summary), as revised and augmented by additional, ongoing research. The figures express the average number of pounds in each currency in that year necessary to buy £100 sterling. They are expressed as whole numbers and decimal fractions in order to make them easier to use in any calculations. Some gaps in the annual averages have been filled by straight-line interpolations based on neighboring data. Interpolated figures are italicized.

APPENDIX C

CURRENCY IN THE UNITED STATES
DURING THE AMERICAN REVOLUTIONARY WAR
AND THE EARLY NATIONAL PERIOD

AFTER A CENTURY AND A HALF during which the currencies used in the Continental Colonies had remained the same in form and remarkably stable in value, the period of the American Revolution brought two momentous changes.[1]

During the war, between 1776 and 1780, the paper currencies issued by the separate states and by the new central government under the Continental Congress depreciated disastrously in value. Across the previous century Americans had slowly introduced paper money into their separate economies beginning with Massachusetts in the 1690s, one colony following the lead of another. Despite—indeed, because of—two separate and limited periods of inflation and one of legislated deflation, their experiments with paper money had been a success. On the eve of the Revolution, all of the colonies had in circulation completely secure, completely satisfactory paper moneys.[2] Thus the wartime inflation came as an unsettling, destabilizing surprise—and required revolutionary changes to repair the damage.[3]

Beginning in 1780, in order to overcome this unhappy experience, the state governments and the central government adopted two related sets of measures. First, they passed laws to withdraw the worthless paper money and to authorize depreciation schedules so that inflated wartime sums of money could be regularized and accounts settled to an agreed standard. Then they passed other laws that set up a new money of account, with a different name, a different system of counting, and a different notational scheme—the standard for their depreciation tables—

1. One reason for that steadiness was the close connection between colonial moneys of account and the money of the Mother Country, the sterling money of Great Britain which was itself steadfast and secure. See Appendix B, above. I am grateful to Dr. Elizabeth M. Nuxoll for reading and commenting on an early draft of this appendix.

2. McCusker and Menard, *The Economy of British America, 1607–1789*, 2d ed., 337–41 and the sources cited there.

3. The United States was not the only country forced by the war to resort to a depreciated paper currency as a means of paying for its expenses. By June 1782, Spain had in circulation nearly $15,000,000 in '*vales*'; by October, they were worth less than 80 percent of their face value. Hamilton, *War and Prices in Spain, 1651–1800*, 77–85.

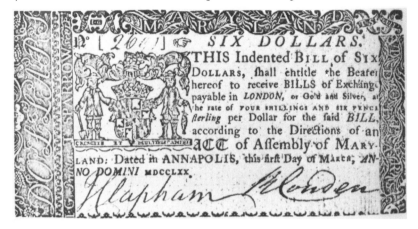

Fig. C-1. A Maryland $6 Bill, 1774 (obverse). It is notable for being denominated in dollars, as had been all of the colony's paper money from 1767 on. Maryland was the first colony to do so. See Newman, *The Early Paper Money of America*, 145 ff. Note that the bill indicates the sterling par for dollars, 4s 6d, on its face. At par, it would have circulated in the colony at £2 5s 0d Maryland 'common currency' (hard currency). McCusker, *Money and Exchange in Europe and America, 1600–1775: A Handbook*, [2d ed., 1992], 189–204. Courtesy, American Antiquarian Society.

the dollar. With the help of these measures, and the eventual return of a more prosperous economy, the period of monetary turmoil gave way to the more settled and satisfactory era of the stable, federal dollar.[4] Both of these developments deserve fuller explanation.

Because the depreciation in the purchasing power of the paper currency of the American Revolutionary War period was a concern for contemporaries and because it has caused confusion for historians, it is worth specifying the relationship between that currency and the currency values that constitute the basis of the commodity price index (the silver dollar). In order to differentiate it from colonial currency, the paper money issued during the American Revolutionary War by the states and by the central government, the Continental Congress, was denominated

4. I am, of course, glossing over the considerable and quite significant monetary difficulties of the middle and late 1780s that contributed greatly to the adoption of the new Constitution. For them, see Alan Nevins, *The American States during and after the Revolution, 1775–1789* (New York: Macmillan Co., 1927). Compare Arthur J. Rolnik, Bruce D. Smith, and Warren E. Weber, 'The Origins of the Monetary Union in the United States,' in *Varieties of Monetary Reforms: Lessons and Experiences on the Road to Monetary Union*, ed. Pierre L. Siklos (Boston: Kluwer Academic Publishers, [1994]), 323–49.

in dollars.[5] At first the paper dollars of the Continental Congress and the states passed, as they were supposed to pass, as the equivalent of the coin after which they were named. One paper dollar was supposed to be —and was, at the start—interchangeable with one hard, silver dollar.

The pressures of war quickly ended that. Some state governments and the Continental Congress, the Federal government, came to print more paper dollars than the economy could bear. Paper money began to lose its worth; all too soon people came to value it at less than they valued the silver dollar (see Table C-1 and Table C-2). As the difference grew, everyone learned to demand and to pay more in paper currency than they did in hard currency. What cost $2.00 if you paid in silver, began to cost $3.00 and then $4.00 if you wanted to pay with paper money.[6] Consequently it became increasingly necessary to specify and then record the difference between the two. So quickly was the paper money issued by the Continental Congress (the 'Continentals') found to be unacceptable that people rarely used it for accounting purposes and some preferred instead to continue to price goods and services in their old colonial moneys of account.[7] Compounding the consequent confusion, each

5. Studies of the money and finance of the period are numerous. Especially valuable is E[lmer] James Ferguson, *The Power of the Purse: A History of American Public Finance, 1776–1790* (Chapel Hill: University of North Carolina Press, 1961). See also Charles J. Bullock, *The Finances of the United States from 1775 to 1789, with Especial Reference to the Budget*, Bulletin of the University of Wisconsin, Economics, Political Science, and History Series, Vol. 1, No. 2 (Madison, Wisconsin: The University, 1895): 131–38. Compare McCusker and Menard, *Economy of British America*, 372–73.

6. David Ramsay, *The History of South-Carolina, from Its First Settlement in 1679, to the Year 1808*, 2 vols. (Charleston, South Carolina: The Author, 1809), 2:99, thought that the attempt by the legislature of South Carolina to prohibit 'any person from receiving or demanding for any article a larger sum in paper than in specie' was 'no less ineffectual' than 'a law to prevent the ebbing and flowing of the sea.'

7. See, e.g., Winifred B[arr] Rothenberg, 'The Emergence of a Capital Market in Rural Massachusetts, 1730–1838,' *Journal of Economy History*, 45 (December 1985): 808, based on her examination of several hundred decedent accounts from the agricultural hinterlands of Boston. Compare Robert Morris summarizing the experiences of the mercantile community: 'It is true that Dollars form our general Circulation but they are not any where the Money of Account. No Merchants Books are kept in Dollars. . . .' Morris, at Philadelphia, to Thomas Jefferson, at Philadelphia, May 1, 1784, in *The Papers of Robert Morris, 1781–1784*, ed. E[lmer] James Ferguson et al., 9 vols. (Pittsburgh, Pennsylvania: University of Pittsburgh Press, 1973–1999), 9:299. By contrast, see Elizabeth Cometti, 'Inflation in Revolutionary Maryland,' *William and Mary Quarterly*, 3d Ser., 8 (April 1951): 228–34, who misread references to Maryland 'common currency' as Marylanders use of 'continental currency.' She mistook the one for the other, perhaps because of the great depreciation in the value of Maryland common currency, but the account book entries she cited were in pounds, shillings, and pence and, thus, in Maryland currency. 'Continentals' were denominated in dollars—as Morris made clear. See also Nevins, *The American States*, 37–49.

state's paper money behaved somewhat differently from that issued by its neighbors and from Congress's 'Continentals.' As confusion bred chaos, Congress finally acted and declared that, as of mid-March 1780, the paper money used during the previous five years would no longer be recognized as legal tender in the country. While some of the paper 'Continentals' continued to circulate in daily transactions—and indeed continued in some places to depreciate in their worth—after the middle of 1780, prices and wages were expressed and transactions settled only in specie value terms, either in the state monies of account (pounds, shillings, and pence) or in Spanish silver dollars.[8]

In an attempt to offset some of the difficulties and inequities that re-sulted from the five years of inflation, several states passed laws and is-sued regulations setting out the progressive deterioration in the value of paper money.[9] Then attempts were made to draw this information to-

8. For two contemporary reports of what happened, see, first, the letter of Gouveneur Morris, at Philadelphia, to the unofficial agent in the United States of the government of Spain, Francisco Rendón, at Philadelphia, March 5, 1782, in *Papers of Robert Morris*, ed. Ferguson et al., 4:350–59, and the report that Rendón wrote based in large part on Mor-ris's letter, Philadelphia, April 20, 1782, pp. 595–624. Compare the report of the envoy from the Austrian Netherlands, Fréderick Eugène François de Beelen-Bertholff, at Philadelphia, 'concernant . . . [les] monnoyées dans la nouvelle République,' in his letter dated at Philadelphia, to the Ministere Plénipotentiaire, Barbiano de Belgioioso, at Brus-sels, September 10, 1785, in Archives de la Secrétairerie d'État et de Guerre, *SEG* no. 2164, Algemeen Rijksarchief/Archives Générales du Royaume, Brussels, Belgium, and as printed in *Die Berichte des ersten Agenten Österreichs in den Vereinigten Staaten von Amerika, Baron de Beelen-Bertholff an Die Regierung der Österreichischen Niederlande in Brüssel, 1784–1789,* ed. Hanns Schlitter, Fontes Rerum Austriacarum/Œsterreichische Ge-schichts-Quellen, Zwiete Abtheilung: Diplomataria et Acta, 45. Band, Zweite Hälfte (Vienna: F. Tempsky, 1891), 480–95. For an important perspective on all this, see Charles W. Calomiris, 'Institutional Failure, Monetary Scarcity, and the Depreciation of the Con-tinental,' *Journal of Economic History*, 68 (March 1988): 47–68. Compare Ron[ald] [W.] Michener, 'Backing Theories and the Currencies of Eighteenth-Century America,' *Jour-nal of Economic History* 68 (September 1988): 682–92; and Calomiris, 'The Depreciation of the Continental: A Reply,' *ibid.*, 693–98.

9. Many state governments, like Massachusetts (for which see also p. 19, n. 11, above), authorized rates of depreciation using indexes of commodity prices. Compare [New Hampshire, General Court, House of Representatives], *State of New-Hampshire. In the House of Representatives, July 3, 1781. The Committee to Form a Table Or Scale of Depreciation For This State, Reported As Their Opinion, That All Contracts Previous to the Last Day of Janu-ary 1777, Shall Be Considered As Silver and Gold; and All Contracts For Paper Money From the Last Day of January 1777 to the Last Day of June 1781, to Be Computed in the Following Man-ner . . .* ([Exeter, N.H.: Zechariah Fowle, 1781]); [Connecticut, Laws and Statutes], *At a General Assembly of the Governor and Company of the State of Connecticut, Holden at Hartford, on the Second Thursday of October, A.D. 1780. An Act to Ascertain the Current Value of Conti-nental Bills of Credit in Spanish Milled Dollars in This State, and of Contracts Made For the Payment Thereof, in the Several Periods of Its Depreciation* ([Hartford, Conn.: Hudson and Goodwin, 1780]); [South Carolina, Commissioners for Ascertaining the Progressive Depreciation of the Paper Currency], *An Accurate Table, Ascertaining the Progressive Depreciation of the Paper-*

gether, to specify it on a national basis, and to regularize it. The data in
Table C-1 and Table C-2 reproduce contemporary tables of the depreciation of the wartime paper money against silver dollars. The tables
show the changing cost for one hundred silver dollars in the paper monies
issued by the Continental Congress and by the various states. For instance, according to these tables, by December 1778, it took $623 in
South Carolina paper dollars, $600 in Pennsylvania paper dollars or
$681 in Continental paper dollars to buy what could be had for $100 in
silver dollars.[10]

Currency, in the Province of South-Carolina, during the Late Usurpation . . . (Charleston, S.C.:
John Wells, Jr., 1781); and [Georgia, Laws and Statutes], *An Act to Ascertain the Various Periods of Depreciation, for the Government and Regulation of All and Every Person or Persons
Whom the Same May Concern* ([Savannah, Ga.: James Johnston, 1783]). For South Carolina,
see also Ramsay, *History of South-Carolina*, 1:252, 2:97–102, 178–79.
      The Loyalist Claims Commission, at work in London during and after the American
Revolution, also collected and compiled similar data on the depreciation of the value of
money in the United States for use in processing claims for damages by those who stayed
loyal to the Crown and suffered losses thereby. See the several papers on 'Currency' in the
volume titled 'Information and Intelligence Conveyed to the Commissioners to Prevent
Imposition and Fraud,' 1782–1785, 68–75, Exchequer and Audit Department Records,
AO 12/107, 68–75, Public Record Office, London (PRO). For copies of these materials,
see Transcripts of the Manuscript Books and Papers of the Commission of Enquiry into
the Losses and Services of the American Loyalists, 1783–1790, 1:131–45, Manuscript and
Archives Division, New York Public Library. Many of these reports were written by
George Chalmers (1742–1825), the Scottish-born antiquary and one-time Maryland
lawyer who, having returned to London in 1775, held the position of chief clerk of the
Board of Trade from 1785 to his death in 1825. Over his lifetime he amassed an immense
collection of books and papers dealing with the United States. See Grace Amelia Cockroft,
The Public Life of George Chalmers, Columbia University, Studies in History, Economics and
Public Law, No. 454 (New York: Columbia University Press, 1939). For a rough draft of
his account of depreciation in Maryland, see Maryland, Vol. 2, fol. 2, George Chalmers Papers, 1606–1812, New York Public Library. See also a copy of Chalmers's 'Anecdotes of
the Depreciation of Paper Currency in the Middle Colonies, during the late Rebellion
[1783],' in American Papers, 2, fol. 94r, Jared Sparks Manuscripts, Houghton Library,
Harvard University, Cambridge, Massachusetts.
      10. Compare the figures published in *The Complete Counting House Companion* (Philadel-
phia), August 20, 1785, 3; and Pelatiah Webster, *Political Essays on the Nature and Operation
of Money, Public Finances, and Other Subjects: Published during the American War, and Continued to the Present Year, 1791* (Philadelphia: Joseph Crukshank, 1791), 501–2. See also, Bullock, *Finances of the United States*, 133; and Bezanson et al., *Prices and Inflation during the
American Revolution*, 58–72 and passim. Ferguson, *Power of the Purse*, 68–69, made the valid
point that these official tables of depreciation understated the full extent of paper money's
loss of purchasing power. But see Webster, loc. cit. For examples of how merchants and
others dealt with all this on a day-to-day basis, see Bezanson et al., 24–57.
      We know that the depreciation schedules were employed in practice from such evidence
as the account of Elnathan Jones, the executor of the will of Hannah Cordis. In it, he reduced sums expressed in the increasingly inflated Massachusetts current money to Massachusetts Lawful Money over the period February 1777 to March 1783 using the rates stip-
ulated in the legal schedules cited above (and reported here in Table C-1, col. 2). (He made
one mistake in his calculations for September 1777.) See the 'Accot. [of] Amts. received

TABLE C-1

AMERICAN REVOLUTIONARY WAR CURRENCY
DEPRECIATION TABLES:
THE NUMBER OF DOLLARS IN FEDERAL AND STATE CURRENCY
EQUAL TO ONE HUNDRED SILVER DOLLARS, 1777–1781

Year Month	Continental Currency	Massachusetts New Hampshire Rhode Island Currency	New York Currency	Pennsylvania Currency	New Jersey Currency
	1	2	3	4	5
January 1777	100	105	100	150	120
February	100	107	100	150	195
March	100	109	100	200	210
April	100	112	100	250	310
May	100	115	100	250	410
June	100	120	100	250	200
July	100	125	100	300	225
August	100	150	100	300	250
September	104	175	102	300	275
October	115	275	112	300	300
November	126	300	124	300	300
December	138	310	136	400	300
January 1778	152	325	149	400	400
February	168	350	164	500	400
March	186	375	181	500	400
April	214	400	209	600	500
May	245	400	238	500	500
June	282	400	273	400	500
July	322	425	318	400	500
August	371	450	359	500	500
September	429	475	415	500	500
October	500	500	482	500	500
November	585	545	565	600	600
December	681	634	655	600	700
January 1779	796	742	769	800	800
February	932	868	909	1,000	1,000

Year Month	Continental Currency	Massachusetts New Hampshire Rhode Island Currency	New York Currency	Pennsylvania Currency	New Jersey Currency
	1	2	3	4	5
March	1,046	1,000	1,024	1,050	1,200
April	1,159	1,104	1,130	1,700	1,600
May	1,271	1,215	1,246	2,400	2,000
June	1,403	1,342	1,374	2,000	2,000
July	1,544	1,477	1,517	1,900	2,000
August	1,705	1,630	1,670	2,000	2,400
September	1,904	1,800	2,021	2,400	2,400
October	2,147	2,030	2,142	3,000	3,000
November	2,432	2,308	2,387	3,850	3,600
December	2,744	2,593	2,669	4,150	4,000
January 1780	3,107	2,934	3,024	4,050	4,200
February	3,519	3,322	3,433	4,750	5,000
March	3,954	3,736	3,866	6,150	6,000
April	4,000	4,200		6,150	6,000
May		5,300		5,900	6,000
June		6,700		6,150	6,000
July		6,950		6,450	6,000
August		7,000		7,000	6,000
September		7,100		7,200	6,000
October		7,200		7,200	7,500
November		7,300		7,400	7,500
December		7,433		7,500	7,500
January 1781		7,467		7,500	7,500
February		7,500		7,500	9,000
March		8,000		12,500	10,000
April		8,500		16,000	12,000
May		9,000		22,500	15,000
June		10,000			
July					
August					
September					
October					
November					
December					

TABLE C-2

AMERICAN REVOLUTIONARY WAR CURRENCY
DEPRECIATION TABLES:
THE NUMBER OF DOLLARS IN FEDERAL AND STATE CURRENCY
EQUAL TO ONE HUNDRED SILVER DOLLARS, 1777–1781

Year Month	Maryland Currency	Virginia Currency	North Carolina Currency	South Carolina Currency
	1	2	3	4
January 1777	150	150	100	100
February	150	150	100	100
March	200	200	125	100
April	250	250	150	108
May	250	250	150	117
June	250	250	175	125
July	300	300	200	139
August	300	300	213	152
September	300	300	225	166
October	300	300	250	186
November	300	300	250	206
December	400	400	300	226
January 1778	400	400	350	221
February	500	500	350	211
March	500	500	375	267
April	600	500	400	317
May	500	500	400	328
June	400	500	400	347
July	400	500	400	354
August	500	500	425	361
September	500	500	450	380
October	500	500	475	405
November	600	600	500	520
December	600	600	550	629
January 1779	800	800	600	761
February	1,000	1,000	650	832
March	1,000	1,000	750	893
April	1,700	1,600	1,000	966
May	2,400	2,000	1,000	832
June	2,000	2,000	1,225	1,177

Year Month	Maryland Currency	Virginia Currency	North Carolina Currency	South Carolina Currency
	1	2	3	4
July	2,000	2,100	1,500	1,457
August	2,000	2,200	1,800	1,637
September	2,400	2,400	2,100	1,618
October	3,000	2,800	2,500	2,040
November	3,850	3,600	2,700	2,596
December	4,150	4,000	3,000	3,233
January 1780	4,000	4,200	3,200	3,775
February	4,700	4,500	3,500	4,217
March	6,000	5,000	4,000	4,659
April	6,000	6,000	5,000	5,101
May	6,000	6,000	6,000	5,245
June	6,000	6,500	7,500	
July	6,000	6,500	9,000	
August	6,500	7,000	10,000	
September	7,500	7,200	12,500	
October	8,500	7,300	15,000	
November	9,000	7,400	17,500	
December	10,000	7,500	20,000	
January 1781	11,000	7,500	21,000	
February	12,000	8,000	22,500	
March	14,000	9,000	25,000	
April	16,000	10,000	26,000	
May	28,000	15,000	30,000	
June	28,000	25,000	35,000	
July		40,000	40,000	
August		50,000	50,000	
September		60,000	55,000	
October		70,000	60,000	
November		80,000	67,500	
December		100,000	72,500	

NOTES AND SOURCES: The data are as published in [United States, Congress], *American State Papers: Documents, Legislative and Executive, of the Congress of the United States*, 38 vols. (Washington, D.C.: Gales and Seaton, 1832–1861), Class III: *Finance*, 5:766–74. See also Henry Phillips, Jr., *Historical Sketches of the Paper Currency of the American Colonies, prior to the Adoption of the Federal Constitution*, 2 vols. (Roxbury, Massachusetts: W. Elliot Woodward, 1865), 2:206–18. The value for Continental currency is the one from the 15th of each month; the value for New York currency is the mean of the values given. Three of the numbers for Massachusetts currency are estimates derived as straight-line interpolations based on data for the neighboring months; they are italicized.

Recall that the fluctuations recorded in the commodity price index in Table A-1, Column 6, are expressed in hard dollars (specie value). Thus it is necessary to convert a sum stated in Pennsylvania paper money (or any of the other paper moneys in use at the time) to silver dollars, using Table C-1, before reducing it to any constant value using the commodity price index in Table A-1.

By the end of the American Revolution the movement was under way to create the new country's own money, a coinage and a money of account based on the Spanish dollar but Americanized to send the message of the new nation. The new decimalized federal dollar was introduced to replace the plethora of colonial pounds, shillings, and pence and a twelve-based system of counting.[11] It was fixed as the money of the United States, the Federal currency, but it was obviously and purposely related to and the equivalent in value to the Spanish dollar, the piece of eight, the *peso de ocho reales*, a Spanish coin, minted in Spain and at the mints that Spain set up for this purpose in the New World. It was, as its name states, the equivalent in the Spanish counting system to eight *reales*, popularly called 'bits' in the English-speaking world, two of which—'two bits'—were a quarter of a dollar, memorialized in 'the good old days' as the price of a shave and a haircut.[12] The coin had a venerable history and, largely because of the long-time stability of its value, by the eighteenth century it was the usual coin of commerce in the Atlantic World. 'Destined to serve as universal money' in Europe, the Western Hemisphere, and much of the modern world, too, as suggested by Aloïss Heiss, historian of Spain's money, the dollar's adoption by the United States as its money was simply one more step in the completion of that conquest—a trend towards 'dollarization' that continues into the

---

by Elnathan Jones from the Estate [of] Hannah Cordis,' May 23, 1775–May 27, 1784, Hannah Cordis Probate Record, File No. 5183, Middlesex County Probate Records, 1648–1871, Massachusetts Judicial Archives, Massachusetts State Archives, Boston, Mass.

11. Initial proposals called for the dollar to have ninety sub-units. Ultimately it was established as a decimalized currency and subdivided into tenths and hundredths of a dollar. The former was supported by Robert Morris; the latter by Thomas Jefferson. See Morris, at Philadelphia, to Jefferson, at Philadelphia, May 1, 1784, in *Papers of Robert Morris*, ed. Ferguson et al., 9:299–302; and Jefferson to Morris, ca. May 7–9, 1784, 9:323–24. Compare, 9:141, n. 3. Between 1783 and 1785 one Philadelphia business newspaper, John Macpherson's *Philadelphia Price Current*, quoted prices in dollars and ninetieths of a dollar because 'Pennsylvania Currency [is] not understood in all Parts of Europe, &c.' See, e.g., *The Philadelphia Price Current*, November 28, 1785.

12. Shepard Pond, 'The Spanish Dollar: The World's Most Famous Silver Coin,' *Bulletin of the Business Historical Society*, 15 (February 1941): 12–16.

twenty-first century.[13] As Thomas Jefferson concluded in 1784 in his preliminary thoughts arguing for its adoption: the 'Dollar is a known coin, and the most familiar of all to the mind of the people. It is already adopted from South to North. . . . Happily the Dollar is familiar to them all; and is already as much referred to for a measure of value as their respective provincial [i.e., State] pounds.'[14] Robert Morris, superintendent of finance, concurred: of 'the Various Coins which have circulated in America . . . there is hardly any which can be considered a general Standard, unless it be Spanish dollars.'[15]

13. Aloïss Heiss, *Descripción general de las monedas hispano-cristianas desde la invasión de los Árabes*, 3 vols. (Madrid: R. N. Milagro, 1865–1869), 1:137, as translated by William Graham Sumner, 'The Spanish Dollar and the Colonial Shilling,' *American Historical Review*, 3 (July 1898): 609. See, especially, Robert Chalmers, *A History of Currency in the British Colonies* (London: Her Majesty's Stationery Office, [1893]), 390–94, 402–3. 'For the entire 351 years from 1497 until 1848, Spanish eight reales minted according to authorized standards, depreciated a meager 4.4% . . . ,' as noted by Philip L. Mossman, *Money of the American Colonies and Confederation: A Numismatic, Economic and Historical Correlation*, Numismatic Studies No. 20 (New York: American Numismatic Society, 1993), 55. Compare Gabriel Calbetó de Grau, *Compendio de las Piezas de Ocho Reales*, 2 vols. (San Juan, Puerto Rico: Ediciones Juan Ponce de Leon, 1970). The 'dollar sign' had evolved by the middle third of the eighteenth century from the abbreviation of the Spanish word peso, 'p^S.' Florian Cajori, *A History of Mathematical Notations*, 2 vols. (Chicago, Ill.: Open Court Publishing Company, [1928–29]), 2:15–29; Alvaro J. Moreno, *El Signo $ de Pesos ¿Cuál es su Origen y qué Representa?* (México: Edición Particular, 1965); Eric P. Newman, 'The Dollar $ign: Its Written and Printed Origins,' in *America's Silver Dollars*, [ed. by John M. Kleeberg], Coinage of the Americas Conference, No. 9 (New York: American Numismatic Society, 1995), 1–49. For the modern discussion of these issues, see Roberto Chang, 'Dollarization: A Scorecard,' *Economic Review—Federal Reserve Bank of Atlanta*, [85] (Third Quarter, 2000), 1–11.

14. 'Jefferson's "Notes on Coinage," [March–May 1784],' *The Papers of Thomas Jefferson*, ed. Julian Boyd et al., in progress (Princeton: Princeton University Press, 1950 to date), 7:175–83 (quot., pp. 177–78). One manuscript version of this text has 'State' where others have 'provincial.' Jefferson's notes were made in the midst of a debate over the details of the project to introduce the new money, as an alternative to some notions being promulgated by Robert Morris. See, especially, Morris, at Philadelphia, to the President of Congress (John Hanson), at Philadelphia, January 15, 1782, *Papers of Robert Morris*, ed. Ferguson et al., 4:25–40. As Jefferson suggested, not only had the states and the central government begun to denominate their currencies in dollars during the war but some colonies, notably Maryland in 1767, had issued currency in dollars even earlier (see Figure C-1). Compare Eric P. Newman, 'The Earliest Money Using the Dollar as an Official Unit of Value,' *The Numismatist*, 98 (November 1985): 2181–87; Newman, *The Early Paper Money of America*, 3d ed. ([Iola, Wisconsin: Krause Publications], 1990), 145 and passim. The American Board of Customs Commissioners, based at Boston, kept its accounts in dollars from 1768 on. See the copy of the Minutes of the Board's meeting, August 30, 1768, enclosed in the letter from Nathaniel Coffin, at Boston, to Charles Steuart, October 28, 1772, Charles Steuart Papers, 1758–1798, MS. 5025, fol. 88, and MS. 5027, fol. 235v, National Library of Scotland, Edinburgh. Coffin was the deputy cashier and paymaster-general of the Customs.

15. Morris to the president of Congress, January 15, 1782, *Papers of Robert Morris*, ed. Ferguson et al., 4:36.

Working out the details of these changes took time. Debates and discussions about the form and gait of this new money lasted through the 1780s and into the early 1790s but, as Jefferson's statement suggests, the dollar was an early odds-on favorite. This was so despite its being the money of account and the real money of another government, Spain, one consequence of which was that the United States had no control over the design of the coin, the denomination in which it was issued, or the quantity produced. Nonetheless, however potent such objections might have been in the colonial period, they could, with due deliberation, be overcome in the new nation. On July 6, 1785, Congress voted that 'the money unit of the United States of America be one dollar.'[16] Even though it went on to approve the decimalized denominations of a coinage a year later, on August 8, 1786, only with the passage of the Mint Act of 1792 and the Coinage Act of 1793 did the United States begin to mint its own coins.[17]

In the meanwhile, however, the relationship between the dollar and the old state moneys of account was already firmly established, something accomplished effectively well before the end of the Revolutionary War. While there would be places where people would continue to refer to shillings and pence down into the middle of the nineteenth century, the relationship between the old Maryland or the old New York money of account and the 'new,' hard dollar was fixed in statute law, unvarying, and commonly known from the 1770s onwards. This was largely because, in setting up the dollar as the new money of account, the states had simply taken over the older, legal valuation of the dollar (the

16. [United States, Continental Congress], *Journals of the Continental Congress, 1774–1789*, ed. Worthington Chauncey Ford et al., 34 vols. (Washington, D.C.: United States Government Printing Office, 1904–37), 29:499–500.

17. *Journals of the Continental Congress, 1774–1789*, 31:503–4. See the 'Act Establishing a Mint, and Regulating the Coins of the United States,' April 2, 1792, ch. 16, and the 'Act Regulating Foreign Coins, and For Other Purposes,' February 9, 1793, ch. 5, [United States, Laws and Statutes] *The Statutes at Large of the United States of America*, ed. Richard Peters, George Minot, and George P. Sanger, 17 vols. (Boston: Little, Brown and Company, 1845–73), 1:246–51, 300–1. Instrumental in the final realization of these plans was Alexander Hamilton's 'Report on the Establishment of a Mint,' January 28, 1791, for which see *The Papers of Alexander Hamilton*, ed. Harold C. Syrett et al., 26 vols. (New York: Columbia University Press, 1961–79), 7:462–607.

In the 1780s some states also minted their own small denomination coins. See Eric P. Newman, 'Circulation of Pre-U.S. Mint Coppers,' in *America's Copper Coinage, 1783–1857*, [ed. Richard G. Doty], Coinage of the Americas Conference, No. 1 (New York: American Numismatic Society, 1984), 101–16; and Mossman, *Money of the American Colonies and Confederation*, 161–99 and passim.

piece of eight) at the par values decreed in the laws of Great Britain and the several states during the colonial period.[18]

Tables of equivalence between the new Federal dollars, the older colonial currencies expressed in pounds, shillings, and pence, and various coins minted in places as far apart as Hamburg and Mexico City were published regularly in newspapers, as broadsides, and in the periodical and pamphlet literature of the 1780s and 1790s. One such table, from a publication by Joseph Lippincott in 1792 — the year of the Mint Act — is reproduced herein as Figure C-2.[19] It will repay our careful scrutiny.

18. For which, see McCusker, *Money and Exchange in Europe and America, 1600–1775: A Handbook*, [2d ed., 1992], 8, 10 and passim. The standard value of the piece of eight in sterling was 4s 6d over the entire period of early British American history. Compare, e.g., Chalmers, *History of Currency*, 48, n.: 'The recognized sterling equivalent to the piece of eight in the seventeenth century was 4*s*. 6*d*.' Just as the par value for colonial currencies was set by the colonial legislatures, so also was the par value in sterling set by regulations and by law in Great Britain. See, e.g., 'The Par of . . . Coynes . . . ,' November 18, 1651, signed by John Reynolds, Assayer of the Royal Mint, State Paper Office Records, SP 18/16, fols. 213r, 216r, PRO; and the Act of 6 Anne, c. 57 (1707). References in the latter format to English (and, later, British) laws can be traced in [Great Britain, Laws and Statutes], *The Statutes at Large . . . of Great Britain*, ed. Danby Pickering, 46 vols. (Cambridge, England: Cambridge University Press, 1762–1807) down through 1806. See also John Hewitt, *A Treatise upon Money, Coins, and Exchange . . .* , [1st ed.] (London: T[homas] Cox, 1740), 175; [United States, Department of State], *Report of the Secretary of State, upon Weights and Measures*, [by John Quincy Adams], [United States, Congress, 16th Congress., 2d. Session, Senate Documents, Vol. No. 4, Doc. No. 119, Serial Set No. 45; House Documents, Vol. No. 8, Doc. No. 109, Serial Set No. 55] (Washington, D.C.: Gales and Seaton, 1821), 143–52; Samuel Moore (Director of the Philadelphia Mint), at Philadelphia, to S[amuel] D. Ingham (Secretary of the Treasury), at Washington, D.C., September 30, 1829, as printed in [International Monetary Conference, 1878, Paris], *Proceedings and Exhibits, Followed by the Report of the American Commission . . .* , [United States, Congress, 45th Congress., 3d. Session, Senate Executive Document No. 58, Serial Set No. 1832] (Washington, D.C.: Government Printing Office, 1879), 603–10; Condy Raguet, *A Treatise on Currency and Banking*, 2nd ed. (Philadelphia: Grigg and Elliot, 1840), 33–35; Mossman, *Money of the American Colonies and Confederation*, 55–56; and Jürgen Schneider et al., *Währungen der Welt*, 14 pts. in 11 vols., Beiträge zur Wirtschafts- und Sozialgeschichte, Nos. 44–50, 57, 59, 61 (Stuttgart: Franz Steiner, 1991–96), 1, pt. i: 232.

19. Lippincott, *A Collection of Tables . . . Shewing the Value of Any Number of Pounds, Shillings and Pence in Dollars and Cents . . .* (Philadelphia: Benjamin Johnson, 1792), [42]. The copy of this book in the Library of Congress, Division of Rare Books and Special Collections, has a hand-written annotation on this page to indicate that the rate that applied for New England and Virginia, 6s currency per dollar, also applied in 'Kentucky, Tennessee, Indiana & Mississippi.' For 'Canada & Nova Scotia,' the rate was 5s currency per dollar. Note three anomalies in the printing of the table, besides the incorrect abbreviation for the state of New York: the printer omitted the heading above the final column (it could have read something like 'Federal Money' or 'Federal Value'); the designation '(silv[er])' next to 'A French Pistole' actually refers to all of the coins below; and the printer mistakenly set the line of figures in the row after the word 'Sweden' that should have been set in the row above, after the word 'Crown.' Compare Table (2) in *The Federal, or New Ready Reckoner . . .* (Chestnut Hill [Philadelphia]: Samuel Sower, 1793); and Chauncey Lee, *The*

A Table of the Weight and Value of Coins as they pass in the respective States of the Union, with their Sterling and Federal value.

Names of Coins	Stand. weight		Ster Mo. of Great Brit.		N.H. M. R.I.C.&/ Virgi.		N. Y. and N. C.		N. Jr. P. Dela. &/ Mary.		South C. and Georgi		Federal value				
	dwt	gr	s	d	s	d	s	d	s	d	s	d	e	d	d	c	m
Gold																	
A Johannes	18	0	3 12	0	4 16	0	6 8	0	6 0	0	4 0	0	1	6	0	0	0
An Half Johannes	9	0	1 16	0	2 8	0	3 4	0	3 0	0	2 0	0		8	0	0	0
A Moidore	6	13	1 7	0	1 16	0	2 8	0	2 5	0	1 8	0		6	0	0	0
A Doubloon	16	21	3 6	0	4 8	0	5 16	0	5 12	6	3 10	0		4	9	3	3
An English Guinea	5	6	1 1	0	1 8	0	1 17	0	1 15	0	1 1	9		4	6	6	7
A French Guinea	5	5	1 1	0	1 7	6	1 16	0	1 14	6	1 1	5		4	6	0	0
A Spanish Pistole	4	6	16	6	1 2	0	1 9	0	1 8	0	0 18	0		3	7	7	3
A French Pistole (silv)	4	4	16	0	1 2	0	1 8	0	1 7	6	0 17	6		3	6	6	7
An Eng. or French Crown	19	0	5	0	6	8	0 8	9	8	4	0 5	0		1	1	1	0
The Dols. of Spain Sweden or Denmark	17	6	4	6	6	0	0 8	0	7	6	0 4	8		1	0	0	0
An English Shilling	3	18	1	0	1	4	0 1	9	1	8	0 1	0		0	2	2	2
A Pistareen	3	11	0	10¾	1	2	0 1	7	1	6	0 0	11		0	2	0	0

Fig. C-2. A Table of the Weight and Value of Coins, 1792. From Joseph Lippincott, *A Collection of Tables* . . . (Philadelphia: Benjamin Johnson, 1792), [42]. Listed are eight gold coins and seven silver coins, their weights in pennyweight and grains, and their values at those weights in the currencies of Great Britain and the various states of the United States as well as in the new federal currency (the last column). See the comments on this table in the text. Courtesy, American Antiquarian Society.

The column listing by name eight gold coins and seven silver ones is followed by the weights of the coins in pennyweight and grains and then the worth of those coins in the 'Ster[ling] Mo[ney]' of Great Brit[ain].' Note especially that the value in British sterling and in the various state currencies of the 'Dol[lar]s of Spain' is at par. Thus the dollar or piece of eight is shown to be equivalent to 4s 6d sterling. For New England—'N[ew] H[ampshire] M[assachusetts] R[hode] I[sland] C[onnecticut]'—'& Virgi[nia],' all of which shared the same legal par, enacted by their separate colonial legislatures, the dollar was at a rate of 6s state currency. This meant that £100 in each of those currencies was the same as $333.33 in the new currency of the United States (compare Table 1).[20] For New York (the 'N.W.' should have been set as 'N.Y.') and 'N[orth] C[arolina]' the dollar was valued at 8s state currency and, consequently,

American Accomptant; Being a Plain, Practical and Systematic Compendium of Federal Arithmetic . . . (Lansingburgh [Troy, New York]: William W. Wands, 1797), 55–56.

20. Computation: If 6s currency equaled $1.00, then £100—or 2,000 shillings—was equal to $333.33 (2,000 ÷ 6 = 333⅓).

£100 state currency was equivalent to $250 federal currency.[21] The states of 'N[ew] J[e]r[sey] P[ennsylvania] Del[aware] [and] Mary[land]' also shared the same par value for the dollar, 7s 6d, and, therefore, £100 in the currency of any one of them equaled $266.67. For 'South C[arolina] and Georgi[a]' the par value of the dollar, at 4s 8d, meant that £100 in their currencies equaled $428.57.[22]

South Carolina was the only state that changed its currency value for the dollar during the Revolutionary War. Over much of the colonial period, from the 1730s onward, the piece of eight had had a value at par of 31s 6d South Carolina currency. In the early 1770s it was increased to 32s 6d, at which rate the colony and state continued to operate during the rest of the decade. Paper money issued during the American Revolution was denominated in both pounds currency and dollars at that rate (e.g., the $8.00 bill authorized on October 19, 1776 stated that it was the equivalent of £13 'Current Money').[23] David Ramsay tells us that, from May 1780 through December 1782, 'while the British were in possession of Charlestown, their sterling was the money of account.'[24] Thus, during that period, the dollar was worth 4s 6d sterling, temporarily the currency of the colony. At the end of the war, as of March 16, 1783, the state legislature reestablished a state currency, this time at a rate of 4s 8d per dollar.[25] Across this entire time the dollar itself remained the same,

21. See, again, Table (2) in *The Federal, or New Ready Reckoner*.

22. See contemporary accounts of these same relationships in, e.g., Samuel Freeman, *A Valuable Assistant to Every Man: or, the American Clerk's Magazine*, 2d ed. (Boston: I[saiah] Thomas and E[benezer] T. Andrews, 1795), 229–34. Compare Nicholas Pike, *A New and Complete System of Arithmetic, Composed for the Use of the Citizens of the United States*, [1st ed.] (Newburyport, Mass.: John Mycall, 1788), 376–78; and Joseph Chaplin, *The Trader's Best Companion: Containing Various Arithmetical Rules . . . Applied to the Federal Currency . . .* (Newburyport, Mass.: William Barrett, 1795), 3, 32. Compare Morris to the President of Congress, January 15, 1782, *Papers of Robert Morris*, ed. Ferguson et al., 4:36.

23. McCusker, *Money and Exchange*, 220–26, esp. 220, n. 212. Compare Ramsay, *History of South-Carolina*, 2:164, 182–83. See also Newman, *Early Paper Money of America*, 416–17.

24. Ramsay, *History of South-Carolina*, 2:183. Compare Arthur Harrison Cole, *Wholesale Commodity Prices in the United States, 1700–1861*, 2 vols. (Cambridge: Harvard University Press, 1938), 2:72–75.

25. [South Carolina, Laws and Statutes], *The Statutes at Large of South Carolina*, ed. Thomas Cooper and David J. McCord, 10 vols. (Columbia, South Carolina: A. S. Johnston, 1836–1841), 4:543. Compare Ramsay, *History of South-Carolina*, 2:183. Concerning that law, passed March 12, 1783, see also the resolution passed by the Charleston Chamber of Commerce on October 17, 1785, reinforcing the monetary standards established in the 1783 law. The resolution was reported in *The Pennsylvania Packet, and Daily Advertiser* (Philadelphia), November 28, 1785. October 1785 was the month when South Carolina inaugurated its first state paper currency. *Statutes at Large*, ed. Cooper and McCord, 4:712–16. It was denominated in South Carolina currency.

its purchasing power constant. What changed from currency to currency was the price paid in those currencies for a dollar. The consequent confusion simply created an additional incentive for the adoption of the dollar itself as the currency of the new nation.

The final column in the table in Figure C-2 specifies in the new Federal currency the values of each of the same coins and tells us, thereby, the ratios that are used in the calculations above. The figures in that column are not headed '£' 's' 'd' for pounds, shillings and pence but are labeled in terms of the new, decimalized Federal currency: 'e[agles],' 'd[ollars],' 'd[imes],' 'c[ents],' and 'm[ills].' All are in the ratio of ten to one, i.e., ten mills equaled one cent, ten dollars, one eagle, and so forth. Thus the gold guinea of Great Britain equaled $4.77 and $\frac{7}{10}$ths.[26] Note, once again, that the Spanish dollar was co-equal with the Federal dollar.

If effecting the changes took some time, their acceptance took far longer. In many places people continued into the nineteenth century to

---

In part because of linguistic inertia, even after the state introduced the new valuation for South Carolina currency, people there continued to refer to their currency as 'sterling.' South Carolinians were no longer using British money, however; they just called it that. The close correspondence between the value of pieces of eight in the currency of Great Britain, where they were rated at 4s 6d each, and the new value for pieces of eight in South Carolina, 4s 8d each, certainly encouraged the retention of the name. Common usage reinforced the practice. The difference in valuations meant a par of exchange of £103.70 South Carolina pounds per £100 pounds sterling of Great Britain. When bills of exchange traded in South Carolina at a 'discount' of 3.75%, a seller of a £100 sterling bill received £100 currency. (See letters from Robert Hazlehurst and Company, at Charleston, to Daniel Parker, at New York, February 7, April 7, April 16, and May 16, 1784, in the Daniel Parker Papers, 1777–1812, Massachusetts Historical Society, Boston. I am very grateful to Dr. Elizabeth M. Nuxoll for these references.) As a consequence we find that South Carolinians used the name 'sterling' in reference to their post-March 1783 currency when they bought and sold real estate. See Brent H. Holcomb, *South Carolina Deed Abstracts [1773–1788]*, 3 vols. ([Columbia, South Carolina: SCMAR, 1993–1996]), 3, passim. They were not actually negotiating property transactions in the money of another country, however. This becomes very clear when, occasionally, someone spelled out exactly what he meant by South Carolina 'sterling.' See, as an example, the terms of the bond dated January 21 and 22, 1785, in the 'sum of £800 sterling money in gold or silver specie at the rate of four shillings and eight pence to the dollar or one pound one shilling and nine pence to the guinea.' *South Carolina Deed Abstracts [1773–1788]*, 76, and compare p. 100 (October 6, 1784). During the 1780s, local transactions in South Carolina denominated in 'sterling' meant, in effect, 'South Carolina sterling,' temporarily another name for 'South Carolina state currency.'

26. Almost a decade earlier, the 'Bank of New-York' notified prospective customers that it would receive and pay out guineas at $4.67. See its 'Rules' published in the *New York Packet*, June 7, 1784. Compare Oscar G. Schilke and Raphael E. Solomon, *America's Foreign Coins: An Illustrated Standard Catalogue with Valuations of Foreign Coins with Legal Tender Status in the United States, 1793–1857* (New York: Coin and Currency Institute, 1964), 188.

set the value of goods and services in the old colonial and state moneys of account, even though as Chauncey Lee observed in 1797, they 'are giving way to one uniform currency of the *Federal Money*.'[27] Those who chose to continue using one or another of the old moneys of account could do so knowing that the relationship between them and the new federal currency was fixed in law and unvarying in practice. Thus when a New Englander in the early nineteenth century valued something at a shilling, every one of his or her neighbors was aware that there were six shillings to a dollar and, if he or she agreed to pay someone three shillings, both knew they would settle the debt with half a dollar.

New Yorkers resisted the change longer than others. They persisted in the old units of account because of the convenient congruence of the old with the new. There were eight New York shillings to the dollar just as there had been eight *reales*, or bits, to the *peso do ocho reales*, the piece of eight. Thus two shillings New York currency were a quarter of a dollar ('two bits'), four shillings were fifty cents ('four bits'), and so forth.[28]

27. Lee, *American Accomptant*, 55. Compare Ramsay, *History of South-Carolina*, 2:183— writing in 1808: 'Several even now keep their accounts in pounds shillings and pence: but a dollar is the legal money unit of the state, and is by degrees becoming the money of account with all the people.'

28. With reference to the 1830s, John Bach McMaster, *A History of the People of the United States from the Revolution to the Civil War*, 8 vols. (New York: D. Appleton, 1883–1913), 1:189–90, testified to the diversity of money systems, the richness of language, and the potential for confusion that characterized commerce in the United States from the 1780s through 1857:

In New York and North Carolina, where eight shillings made a dollar, the eighth was a shilling, and went by that name. From New Jersey to Maryland the same coin was nearly equalled by eleven pence, and was called the eleven-penny-bit or the levy; but became for a like reason, nineteen pence in New England. In the same way the sixteenth of a dollar was called sixpence in New York, five-penny-bit, or the fip, in Pennsylvania, and fourpence in New England. In Louisiana, the people called it the picayune. Sixpence, in Massachusetts, meant eight and a third cents; a shilling meant sixteen and two thirds cents; two and threepence was thirty-seven and a half cents; three shillings was fifty cents; four and six was seventy-five cents; nine shillings was a dollar and a half. A merchant, therefore, in place of asking twenty-five cents for a yard of the taffeta or a pound of his cheese would have demanded one and six, a price which the purchaser of the taffeta or cheese would, if he were so disposed, have paid by putting down the silver coin familiar to us as the quarter of a dollar. Some shilling pieces and sixpence pieces were to be found in circulation even to the civil war, and were, with the fips, the levies, and the pistareens, the last relics of a time happily passed away.

Until the end of the nineteenth century, according to Martha W. Hiden, Virginians used the phrase 'ni'pence' (nine pence) to mean half-a-quarter ($12\frac{1}{2}$ cents) and the word 'shilling' to mean $16\frac{2}{3}$ cents. Thus country storekeepers sold butter for 'a shilling a pound, three pounds for 50 cents.' Mrs. Philip Wallace Hiden, 'The Money of Colonial Virginia,' *Virginia Magazine of History and Biography*, 51 (January 1943): 48.

In 1845, the leading commercial newspaper of the time, *Niles' Register*, editorialized:[29]

> It is a curious fact, that whilst the present generation in Maryland, Virginia, and indeed almost the whole of the Union besides, hardly know how many *shillings* and *pence* a dollar used to be rated at under their old colonial governments, and now never use the terms in any of their business transactions, the people of the great emporium of trade,—the city and state of New York, continue to keep accounts and buy and sell by *shillings* and *pence* instead of dollars and cents! . . . . We recognize a person in a moment as from the 'New Netherlands,' or as a 'down easter' that asks so many *shillings* for his commodity, and invariably make him Americanize, by translating the amount into dollars and cents.

So powerful was this tradition that only a century and a half later, on the eve of a new millennium, did the most sophisticated of all New York financial institutions, the New York Stock Exchange, change the way in which it had valued and traded shares of stock for over two hundred years. In response to an order from the United States Securities and Exchange Commission (SEC), over the eight months from August 2000 to April 2001, the Exchange finally abandoned its usage of dollars and bits—dollars and eighths of a dollar—and adopted the decimalized format long in common use by everyone else.[30]

---

29. *Niles' National Register* (Baltimore), January 11, 1845. The editors also noted that 'until a few years ago *tobacco* was the legal currency of Maryland, and that all accounts for taxes, legal fees, &c had to be kept and rendered, not in dollars and cents, or pounds, shillings or pence either, but in so many pounds of tobacco. . . . We have no recollection of having seen an account rendered in pounds, shillings, and pence, Maryland currency, within the last twenty years,—though within the period, if memory deceives not, we have paid fee bills rendered in the tobacco currency.' Compare 'The Provincial Currency of Maryland,' *[Fisher's] National Magazine and Industrial Record*, 2 (January 1846): 690–94.

30. *The New York Times*, August 22, 2000. On that date, in anticipation of the change, the newspaper converted its stock market tables to dollars and cents. The SEC ruling applied to all securities exchanges in the United States and was to be in effect by April 9, 2001.

Contrast the action announced by the Philadelphia Stock Exchange on November 1, 1800. 'As there are no such coins in the United States, as pounds, shillings, and pence, the Brokers of Philadelphia in future, intend to buy and sell all kinds of Publick Stock, at so much per cent. in Dollars and Cents, which are the proper coins of the United States, and not as heretofore, at so much per pound.' *New-York Price-Current*, November 29, 1800.

APPENDIX D

COMMODITY PRICE INDEXES,
GREAT BRITAIN, 1600–2000

THAT THE AMERICAN COLONISTS were subjects of Great Britain, that the economies of the colonies and the Mother Country were interconnected, even interdependent, and that the economies of Great Britain and the United States continue to have a 'special relationship' down into the twenty-first century suggests a possible comparative element to any discussion of the commodity price index in the United States from the first days of the colonial period to today.

Even more commodity price indexes have been compiled for Great Britain than for the United States.[1] Again, however, others have done the job of sorting through them and have selected those most useful for purposes of historical analysis. Michael W. Flinn compared them all and concluded: 'The study of these indexes immediately brings out one feature that encourages one to take a slightly more positive attitude to them: that is their quite remarkable degree of agreement. Whatever criticisms might be made against this or that aspect of individual indexes, when juxtaposed it is their similarity of behaviour both in the short and long run that first impresses one.'[2]

If only because it was calculated on the same basis for so long a period and, as a result, satisfies the important criterion of consistency over such a long time, the index of English commodity prices used by most economic historians is the one generated by Ernest H. Phelps Brown and Sheila V. Hopkins. In compiling their index for the early period, Phelps Brown and Hopkins used the price data assembled during the 1930s by Lord Beveridge and his colleagues for the English price history project;

1. For many of them, see Brian R. Mitchell, *British Historical Statistics* (Cambridge: Cambridge University Press, 1988), 714–36. Compare the discussion in Gerald Reitlinger, *The Economics of Taste*, 3 vols. (London: Barrie and Rockliff, 1961–1970), 1:xvi, 2:xii, 3:9–17.

2. Flinn, 'Trends in Real Wages, 1750–1850,' *Economic History Review*, 2d Ser., 27 (August 1974): 402. As Flinn implies, over shorter periods the correspondence may not be quite so compelling. In such circumstances some have compiled and used other indexes. See, e.g., Charles [H.] Feinstein, *Conjectures and Contrivances: Economic Growth and the Standard of Living in Britain during the Industrial Revolution*, Discussion Papers in Economic and Social History, No. 9 ([Oxford]: University of Oxford, [1996]).

for the past two centuries they relied more on the work of others. Their index spanned seven centuries from 1264 to 1954 on a reference base 1451–1475 = 100; for the period 1600 to 1954, it is reproduced here in Table D-1, Column 1.[3] For a comparison with another eighteenth-century commodity price index (reference base 1700–1702), see the one compiled by Elizabeth Boody Schumpeter and Elizabeth W. Gilboy as reproduced in Column 2, Table D-1.[4]

   It is possible to splice the Phelps Brown-Hopkins index into a retail price index compiled monthly by the Office for National Statistics (formerly the Central Statistical Office) and consequently to extend the British commodity price index down to the present. The original series, on a reference base 1967 = 100, is reproduced here in Table D-1, Col-

   3. E[rnest] H. Phelps Brown and Sheila V. Hopkins, 'Seven Centuries of the Prices of Consumables Compared with Builders' Wage-rates,' *Economica*, New Ser., 23 (November 1956): 296–314. This and related essays have been reprinted in Phelps Brown and Hopkins, *A Perspective of Wages and Prices* (London and New York: Methuen, 1981).
   The Phelps Brown and Hopkins index continues to be used by economic historians of Great Britain, although, as has just been said, it has not gone without criticism. See the essay concerning it in E[dward] A. Wrigley and R[oger] S. Schofield, *The Population History of England, 1641–1871: A Reconstruction* (Cambridge, Mass.: Harvard University Press, 1981), 638–41. It does nothing to diminish the potential validity of any criticisms—though it may diminish their force—to indicate not only that Phelps Brown and Hopkins recognized most of the problems themselves but also that many of the criticisms of their index emanate from a dissatisfaction with the results it generates for a particular piece of research. See, e.g., the comments by D[avid] [J.] Loschky, 'Seven Centuries of Real Income per Wage Earner Reconsidered,' *Economica*, New Ser., 47 (November 1980): 459–65; or Donald [M.] Woodward, 'Wage Rates and Living Standards in Pre-Industrial England,' *Past & Present: A Journal of Historical Studies*, 91 (May 1981): 28–46. Compare H[arold] F. Lydall and E[rnest] H. Phelps Brown, 'Seven Centuries of Real Income per Wage-Earner Reconsidered: A Note,' *Economica*, New Ser., 49 (May 1982): 201–5; and [Ernest] Henry Phelps Brown, 'Gregory King's Notebook and the Phelps Brown-Hopkins Price Index,' *Economic History Review*, 2d Ser., 43 (February 1990): 99–103. Jan de Vries, in his usual calm and masterful manner, attempts to resolve some of this by noting that, despite the flaws which everyone knows, this is the tool that we have to work with and we need to make the best we can of it. See his 'Between Purchasing Power and the World of Goods: Understanding the Household Economy in Early Modern Europe,' in *Consumption and the World of Goods*, ed. John Brewer and Roy Potter (London and New York: Routledge, 1993), 96–98.
   4. [Romaine] Elizabeth Boody Schumpeter, 'English Prices and Public Finance, 1660–1822,' *Review of Economic Statistics*, 20 (1938): 21–37, and Elizabeth W. Gilboy, 'The Cost of Living and Real Wages in Eighteenth Century England,' *Review of Economic Statistics*, 18 (1936): 134–43. Averaged here are the two authors' wholesale commodity price indexes for producers' goods and consumers' goods. Compare Phyllis Deane and W[illiam] A. Cole, *British Economic Growth, 1688–1959: Trends and Structure*, 2d ed. (Cambridge: Cambridge University Press, 1969), 14, and Figure 7; and John J. McCusker, 'The Current Value of English Exports, 1697 to 1800,' *William and Mary Quarterly*, 3d Ser., 28 (October 1971): 607–28, as revised and amended in McCusker, *Essays in the Economic History of the Atlantic World* (London: Routledge, 1997), 617–19. The original Schumpeter-Gilboy indexes are reprinted in Mitchell, *British Historical Statistics*, 719–20.

umn 3.[5] Table D-1, Column 4, is a composite index combining the Phelps Brown-Hopkins series and the Office for National Statistics series. Linkage is accomplished at 1954. The reference base for Column 4 is the same as that for Table A-1, Column 6, 1860 = 100.

An intriguing question for economic historians of early America is just how closely the index numbers in Table D-1, Column 4, correlate with those in Table A-1, Column 6. The answer is: quite well indeed (see Figure 1). Much that Michael Flinn is quoted above as stating about the relationships among British commodity price indexes could also be said about the connections between the British and the American commodity price indexes. For the period 1665 to 1860 the two moved in parallel tracks. They changed direction at roughly the same times and to roughly the same degree. Such parallels continued to operate through the end of the nineteenth and into the twentieth centuries. Indeed, given the close connections between the two economies and the workings of such mechanisms as commercial and financial arbitrage, these parallels are to be expected, especially during the Old Empire.[6]

5. Prices are normally collected on the Tuesday nearest the 15th of the month, then compiled, and the index number released for any one month midway into the next month. The monthly figures (currently on a reference base January 1987 = 100) are issued to the press and later published in the monthly editions of the *Labour Market Trends* (formerly the *Employment Gazette*; originally [1893], *The Labour Gazette*). Compare Crowe, *Index Numbers*, 155; [Great Britain, Office for National Statistics], *Retail Prices, 1914–1990* (London: Her Majesty's Stationery Office, 1991), 6. See also the pamphlets issued by the ONS, such as *Retail Prices Index: A Brief Guide to the RPI* (London: [Her Majesty's Stationery Office], 1996). In Britain it is possible to obtain the monthly index number over the telephone through the Public Enquiries service of the ONS. Call the ONS in London for recorded information (from the United States, 011-44-20-7-533-5866). The ONS has also set up a website for those with access to the World Wide Web (http://www.ons.gov.uk). The monthly updates are available at http://www.statistics.gov.uk/data1.htm as part of the 'Press Releases' service. Beginning in January 1999 the ONS has also published these data as part of the 'Harmonized Index of Consumer Prices' (HICP) compiled to conform to the methods instituted by the European Central Bank as a means of measuring price stability across the European Union. They are also distributed in a printed form by the Office for National Statistics and are published in its *Monthly Digest of Statistics* (since 1946) and *Economic Trends* (since 1953). Quarterly and annual averages for the past fifteen years are published in [Great Britain, Office for National Statistics], *Annual Abstract of Statistics* (London: Her Majesty's Stationery Office, 1853 to date). The annual series is reproduced (through 1980) in Mitchell, *British Historical Statistics*, 739–41. See, in addition, the monthly, quarterly and annual figures reproduced in the International Monetary Fund's *International Financial Statistics* (monthly).

6. McCusker and Menard, *The Economy of British America, 1607–1789* (2d ed., 1991), 62–64, Table 3.4, make this argument. It has been contended by others as well, although more for the nineteenth than for the seventeenth and eighteenth centuries, when, to my mind, the connections were even closer. See especially T[homas] S. Ashton, *Economic Fluctuations in England, 1700–1800* (Oxford: Clarendon Press, 1959), passim, but notably 172–73. See also the periods of 'good trade,' 'bad trade,' and 'crises,' 1558–1720, defined in

The parallels between the colonial and the British commodity price indexes suggest three things. First, each index gains in credibility. The data for both commodity price indexes and, thus, the index numbers themselves are sound and can be relied upon as reasonably accurate in their depiction of the movement of commodity prices in each place. Second, our appreciation of the reality of the close connections among the economies along the Atlantic rim is buttressed. The British and the British colonial economies were clearly interrelated. The colonists were integrally tied to the Atlantic economy of which Great Britain, by the middle of the eighteenth century, was—with France—one of the two leading powers.[7] Finally, the synchronicity of the two indexes during the late seventeenth and early eighteenth centuries and afterwards suggest that the fluctuations expressed by the British commodity price index in the first two-thirds of the seventeenth century probably described colonial price movements fairly well, for it is also a period for which we do not yet have adequate colonial commodity price indexes.[8]

William Robert Scott, *The Constitution and Finance of English, Scottish, and Irish Joint-Stock Companies to 1720*, 3 vols. (Cambridge: Cambridge University Press, 1911), 1:465–67; and the chronology of labor disputes in Britain, 1717–80, set out in C. R. Dobson, *Masters and Journeymen: A Prehistory of Industrial Relations, 1717–1800* (London: Croom Helm; and Totowa, N.J.: Rowman and Littlefield, [1980]), 154–70. A frequency count of such disputes correlates reasonably well with the business cycle and shows a very slight tendency for more disputes per year in periods of contraction than periods of expansion. Douglas Fisher, *The Industrial Revolution: A Macroeconomic Interpretation* (London: Macmillan, 1992), 35–40, delineates the British business cycle through 1780. The first two studies—Ashton and, to a lesser extent Scott—were the basis for McCusker and Menard, *The Economy of British America, 1607–1789* (2d ed., 1991), Table 3.4 referred to above. Compare the cycles exhibited by prices in the Scottish economy, as in A[lex] J. S. Gibson and T[homas] C[hristopher] Smout, *Prices, Food and Wages in Scotland, 1550–1780* ([Cambridge]: Cambridge University Press, 1995), 164–67. For the nineteenth century, see, e.g., J[onathan] R. T. Hughes and Nathan Rosenberg, 'The United States Business Cycle before 1860: Some Problems of Interpretation,' *Economic History Review*, 2d Ser., 15 (December 1963): 481, 493, and the works they cite, R[obert] C. O. Matthews, *A Study in Trade-Cycle History: Economic Fluctuations in Great Britain, 1833–1842* (Cambridge: Cambridge University Press, 1954), 43–69, 202–24 and passim; J[onathan] R. T. Hughes, *Fluctuations in Trade, Industry, and Finance* (Oxford: Clarendon Press, 1960), 40. See also W[alt] W. Rostow, *The World Economy: History & Prospect* (Austin: University of Texas Press, [1978]), 311, 315 and passim; and Peter Temin, 'Labour Scarcity and Capital Markets in America,' in *Landowners, Capitalists and Entrepreneurs: Essays for Sir John Habakkuk*, ed. F[rancis] M. L. Thompson (Oxford: Clarendon Press, 1994), 257–73, who finds evidence of a single capital market from the 1790s onwards.

7. See, again, McCusker and Menard, *Economy of British America*, 62–64, Table 3.4.

8. For one of the implications of this suggestion, see Appendix A, n. 13, above. Compare Appendix A, n. 18, above.

TABLE D-1

COMMODITY PRICE INDEXES, GREAT BRITAIN, 1600–2000

Year (Base =)	Phelps Brown and Hopkins (1450–1475)	Schumpeter-Gilboy (1700–1702)	Office of National Statistics (1967)	Composite Commodity Price Index (1860)
	1	2	3	4
1600	459			35
1601	536			41
1602	471			36
1603	448			34
1604	404			31
1605	448			34
1606	468			36
1607	449			34
1608	507			39
1609	559			43
1610	503			38
1611	463			35
1612	524			40
1613	549			42
1614	567			43
1615	561			43
1616	562			43
1617	537			41
1618	524			40
1619	494			38
1620	485			37
1621	461			35
1622	523			40
1623	588			45
1624	543			41
1625	534			41
1626	552			42

Year (Base =)	Phelps Brown and Hopkins (1450–1475)	Schumpeter-Gilboy (1700–1702)	Office of National Statistics (1967)	Composite Commodity Price Index (1860)
	1	2	3	4
1627	496			38
1628	466			35
1629	510			39
1630	595			45
1631	682			52
1632	580			44
1633	565			43
1634	611			46
1635	597			45
1636	593			45
1637	621			47
1638	707			54
1639	607			46
1640	546			42
1641	586			45
1642	557			42
1643	553			42
1644	531			40
1645	574			44
1646	569			43
1647	667			51
1648	770			59
1649	821			62
1650	839			64
1651	704			54
1652	648			49
1653	579			44
1654	543			41
1655	531			40
1656	559			43
1657	612			47

Year (Base =)	Phelps Brown and Hopkins (1450–1475)	Schumpeter-Gilboy (1700–1702)	Office of National Statistics (1967)	Composite Commodity Price Index (1860)
	1	2	3	4
1658	646			49
1659	700			53
1660	684			52
1661	648	115		49
1662	769	122		59
1663	675	117		51
1664	657	112		50
1665	616	116		47
1666	664	117		51
1667	577	117		44
1668	602	111		46
1669	572	103		44
1670	577	104		44
1671	595	106		45
1672	557	101		42
1673	585	103		45
1674	650	104		49
1675	691	107		53
1676	652	105		50
1677	592	99		45
1678	633	98		48
1679	614	102		47
1680	568	98		43
1681	567	95		43
1682	600	95		46
1683	587	97		45
1684	570	97		43
1685	651	93		50
1686	559	90		43
1687	580	85		44
1688	551	85		42

Year (Base =)	Phelps Brown and Hopkins (1450–1475)	Schumpeter-Gilboy (1700–1702)	Office of National Statistics (1967)	Composite Commodity Price Index (1860)
	1	2	3	4
1689	535	88		41
1690	513	96		39
1691	493	101		38
1692	542	95		41
1693	652	98		50
1694	693	103		53
1695	645	105		49
1696	697	113		53
1697	693	112		53
1698	767	111		58
1699	773	114		59
1700	671	104		51
1701	586	97		45
1702	582	99		44
1703	551	96		42
1704	587	97		45
1705	548	93		42
1706	583	97		44
1707	531	89		40
1708	571	92		43
1709	697	101		53
1710	798	111		61
1711	889	119		68
1712	638	97		49
1713	594	94		45
1714	635	94		48
1715	646	92		49
1716	645	91		49
1717	602	90		46
1718	575	89		44
1719	609	92		46

Year (Base =)	Phelps Brown and Hopkins (1450–1475)	Schumpeter-Gilboy (1700–1702)	Office of National Statistics (1967)	Composite Commodity Price Index (1860)
	1	2	3	4
1720	635	94		48
1721	604	92		46
1722	554	89		42
1723	525	85		40
1724	589	88		45
1725	610	89		46
1726	637	94		48
1727	596	94		45
1728	649	94		49
1729	681	97		52
1730	599	94		46
1731	553	89		42
1732	557	87		42
1733	544	83		41
1734	518	85		39
1735	529	84		40
1736	539	82		41
1737	581	85		44
1738	563	84		43
1739	547	86		42
1740	644	92		49
1741	712	100		54
1742	631	95		48
1743	579	90		44
1744	518	88		39
1745	528	81		40
1746	594	89		45
1747	574	86		44
1748	599	89		46
1749	609	91		46
1750	590	89		45

Year (Base =)	Phelps Brown and Hopkins (1450–1475)	Schumpeter-Gilboy (1700–1702)	Office of National Statistics (1967)	Composite Commodity Price Index (1860)
	1	2	3	4
1751	574	85		44
1752	601	85		46
1753	585	83		45
1754	615	87		47
1755	578	89		44
1756	602	90		46
1757	733	99		56
1758	731	101		56
1759	673	98		51
1760	643	97		49
1761	614	95		47
1762	638	95		49
1763	655	98		50
1764	713	99		54
1765	738	100		56
1766	747	100		57
1767	790	101		60
1768	781	100		59
1769	717	93		55
1770	714	94		54
1771	775	98		59
1772	858	105		65
1773	855	106		65
1774	863	104		66
1775	815	103		62
1776	797	105		61
1777	794	102		60
1778	826	107		63
1779	756	107		58
1780	730	108		56
1781	760	109		58

Year (Base =)	Phelps Brown and Hopkins (1450–1475)	Schumpeter-Gilboy (1700–1702)	Office of National Statistics (1967)	Composite Commodity Price Index (1860)
	1	2	3	4
1782	776	115		59
1783	869	120		66
1784	874	114		67
1785	839	110		64
1786	839	113		64
1787	834	111		63
1788	867	114		66
1789	856	109		65
1790	871	112		66
1791	870	111		66
1792	883	113		67
1793	908	123		69
1794	978	124		74
1795	1,091	131		83
1796	1,161	142		88
1797	1,045	141		80
1798	1,022	135		78
1799	1,148	140		87
1800	1,567	173		119
1801	1,751	190		133
1802	1,348			103
1803	1,268			96
1804	1,309			100
1805	1,521			116
1806	1,454			111
1807	1,427			109
1808	1,476			112
1809	1,619			123
1810	1,670			127
1811	1,622			123
1812	1,836			140

Year (Base =)	Phelps Brown and Hopkins (1450–1475)	Schumpeter-Gilboy (1700–1702)	Office of National Statistics (1967)	Composite Commodity Price Index (1860)
	1	2	3	4
1813	1,881			143
1814	1,642			125
1815	1,467			112
1816	1,344			102
1817	1,526			116
1818	1,530			116
1819	1,492			114
1820	1,353			103
1821	1,190			91
1822	1,029			78
1823	1,099			84
1824	1,193			91
1825	1,400			107
1826	1,323			101
1827	1,237			94
1828	1,201			91
1829	1,189			90
1830	1,146			87
1831	1,260			96
1832	1,167			89
1833	1,096			83
1834	1,011			77
1835	1,028			78
1836	1,141			87
1837	1,169			89
1838	1,177			90
1839	1,263			96
1840	1,286			98
1841	1,256			96
1842	1,161			88
1843	1,030			78

Year (Base =)	Phelps Brown and Hopkins (1450–1475)	Schumpeter-Gilboy (1700–1702)	Office of National Statistics (1967)	Composite Commodity Price Index (1860)
	1	2	3	4
1844	1,029			78
1845	1,079			82
1846	1,122			85
1847	1,257			96
1848	1,105			84
1849	1,035			79
1850	969			74
1851	961			73
1852	978			74
1853	1,135			86
1854	1,265			96
1855	1,274			97
1856	1,264			96
1857	1,287			98
1858	1,190			91
1859	1,214			92
1860	1,314			100
1861	1,302			99
1862	1,290			98
1863	1,144			87
1864	1,200			91
1865	1,238			94
1866	1,296			99
1867	1,346			102
1868	1,291			98
1869	1,244			95
1870	1,241			94
1871	1,320			100
1872	1,378			105
1873	1,437			109
1874	1,423			108

Year (Base =)	Phelps Brown and Hopkins (1450–1475)	Schumpeter-Gilboy (1700–1702)	Office of National Statistics (1967)	Composite Commodity Price Index (1860)
	1	2	3	4
1875	1,310			100
1876	1,370			104
1877	1,330			101
1878	1,281			97
1879	1,210			92
1880	1,174			89
1881	1,213			92
1882	1,140			87
1883	1,182			90
1884	1,071			82
1885	1,026			78
1886	931			71
1887	955			73
1888	950			72
1889	948			72
1890	947			72
1891	998			76
1892	996			76
1893	914			70
1894	982			75
1895	968			74
1896	947			72
1897	963			73
1898	982			75
1899	950			72
1900	994			76
1901	986			75
1902	963			73
1903	1,004			76
1904	985			75
1905	989			75

Year (Base =)	Phelps Brown and Hopkins (1450–1475)	Schumpeter-Gilboy (1700–1702)	Office of National Statistics (1967)	Composite Commodity Price Index (1860)
	1	2	3	4
1906	1,016			77
1907	1,031			78
1908	1,043			79
1909	1,058			81
1910	994			76
1911	984			75
1912	999			76
1913	1,021			78
1914	1,147			87
1915	1,317			100
1916	1,652			126
1917	1,965			150
1918	2,497			190
1919	2,254			172
1920	2,591			197
1921	2,048			156
1922	1,672			127
1923	1,726			131
1924	1,740			132
1925	1,708			130
1926	1,577			120
1927	1,496			114
1928	1,485			113
1929	1,511			115
1930	1,275			97
1931	1,146			87
1932	1,065			81
1933	1,107			84
1934	1,097			83
1935	1,149			87
1936	1,211			92

Year (Base =)	Phelps Brown and Hopkins (1450–1475)	Schumpeter-Gilboy (1700–1702)	Office of National Statistics (1967)	Composite Commodity Price Index (1860)
	1	2	3	4
1937	1,275			97
1938	1,274			97
1939	1,209			92
1940	1,574			120
1941	1,784			136
1942	2,130			162
1943	2,145			163
1944	2,216			169
1945	2,282			174
1946	2,364			180
1947	2,580			196
1948	2,781			212
1949	3,145			239
1950	3,155			240
1951	3,656			278
1952	3,987			303
1953	3,735			284
1954	3,825		69	291
1955			72	303
1956			74	312
1957			77	324
1958			79	333
1959			79	335
1960			80	339
1961			83	350
1962			85	360
1963			87	367
1964			90	379
1965			94	397
1966			98	412
1967			100	422

Year (Base =)	Phelps Brown and Hopkins (1450–1475)	Schumpeter- Gilboy (1700–1702)	Office of National Statistics (1967)	Composite Commodity Price Index (1860)
	1	2	3	4
1968			105	442
1969			110	466
1970			117	496
1971			129	543
1972			138	582
1973			150	635
1974			174	736
1975			217	915
1976			252	1,066
1977			291	1,231
1978			317	1,338
1979			359	1,517
1980			424	1,789
1981			474	2,002
1982			515	2,174
1983			538	2,274
1984			565	2,387
1985			599	2,532
1986			620	2,619
1987			646	2,728
1988			677	2,862
1989			730	3,084
1990			799	3,376
1991			846	3,574
1992			878	3,707
1993			891	3,765
1994			913	3,859
1995			944	3,990
1996			968	4,089
1997			998	4,216
1998			1,032	4,360

Year (Base =)	Phelps Brown and Hopkins (1450–1475)	Schumpeter-Gilboy (1700–1702)	Office of National Statistics (1967)	Composite Commodity Price Index (1860)
	1	2	3	4
1999			1,048	4,426
2000			1,079	4,559
2001				4,682 (est.)
2002				
2003				
2004				
2005				
2006				
2007				
2008				
2009				

NOTES AND SOURCES: The dates in the column heading are the reference base periods (e.g., 1451–1475 = 100). The figures in Column 1 are from E[rnest] H. Phelps Brown and Sheila V. Hopkins, 'Seven Centuries of the Prices of Consumables Compared with Builder's Wage-rates,' *Economica*, New Ser., 23 (November 1956): 312–14. Column 2 is the average of the two series developed and presented by [Romaine] Elizabeth Boody Schumpeter, 'English Prices and Public Finance, 1660–1822,' *Review of Economic Statistics*, 20 (1938): 21–37, and Elizabeth W. Gilboy, 'The Cost of Living and Real Wages in Eighteenth Century England,' *Review of Economic Statistics*, 18 (1936): 134–43. For Column 3, see the text above and the sources cited in this appendix, n. 5, above, especially [Great Britain, Office for National Statistics], *Annual Abstract of Statistics*, No. 125 (London: Her Majesty's Stationery Office, 1989), 316, and the monthly press releases issued by the Office for National Statistics at it website: http://www.statistics.gov.uk. Column 4 links Column 1 and Column 3 and converts the series to the new reference base period (1860 = 100). Linkage is effected at 1954.

APPENDIX E

PERIODS OF EXPANSION AND CONTRACTION IN THE ECONOMY OF THE UNITED STATES, 1665–1853

COMMODITY PRICE DATA may be used to help identify the phases of the business cycle, at least up to the beginning of the Second World War, as has been discussed in the text, above. The index numbers in Table A-1, Column 6, for the seventeenth, the eighteenth and the first half of the nineteenth centuries are the basis of both Table E-1 (as well as for Figure 1). Between 1665 and 1853 there were forty full cycles of contraction and expansion in the economy of early British America. The average cycle lasted four-and-a-half years, trough to trough and peak to peak (fifty-four months).[1] The two-part trend line over the seventeenth and eighteenth centuries traced, first, the continuation of a long, slow decline that had its beginnings in the mid-seventeenth century and reached its nadir during the 1730s, ending on the eve of King George's War (the War of the Austrian Succession); and, second, a steady rise that continued on into the nineteenth century, peaking at the time of the War of 1812.[2]

1. Between December 1854 and March 1991, the economy of the United States experienced thirty-two cycles that averaged, peak to peak, about fifty-four months in duration according to the National Bureau of Economic Research (NBER). [United States, President], *Economic Report of the President . . . 1999* (Washington, D.C.: United States Government Printing Office, 1999), 21. For this information in detail and the most recent updates, see the website established by the NBER's Business Cycle Dating Committee: http://www.nber.org/cycles.html. Compare Burns and Mitchell, *Measuring Business Cycles*, 78; *Statistical Abstract of the United States*, 109th ed. (1989), 534; 'Business Cycle Expansions and Contractions in the United States,' *Business Conditions Digest*, 30 (January 1990): 104. The most recent peak was in July 1990 and trough in March 1991. See, more generally, Geoffrey H. Moore, 'Business Cycles, Panics, and Depressions,' in *Encyclopedia of American Economic History: Studies of the Principal Movements and Ideas*, 1:151–56, and the sources he cited there; and *Business Cycles and Depressions: An Encyclopedia*, ed. David Glasner (New York: Garland Publishing, 1997), 732–33. For revisionist work on the subject, see Christina D. Romer, 'The Prewar Business Cycle Reconsidered: New Estimates of Gross National Product, 1869–1908,' *Journal of Political Economy*, 93 (February 1989): 1–39; and Mark W. Watson, 'Business-Cycle Durations and Postwar Stabilization of the U.S. Economy,' *American Economic Review*, 84 (March 1994): 24–46.

2. A closer look indicates that the 1660s–1730s decline incorporated a mild recovery that began in the mid-1680s and peaked in the period between King William's War (the War of the League of Augsburg) and Queen Anne's War (the War of the Spanish Succession). The resulting four-part trend-line thus resembled the letter 'W' in its configuration. See McCusker and Menard, *The Economy of British America, 1607–1789* (2d ed., 1991), 67 and passim. Compare A[lex] J. S. Gibson and T[homas] C[hristopher] Smout, *Prices, Food and Wages in Scotland, 1550–1780* ([Cambridge]: Cambridge University Press, 1995), 164–67.

Both the fluctuations and the trends in the business cycle of the pre-Civil War American economy paralleled the fluctuations and trends in the economy of Great Britain (see Appendix D and Figure 1). The parallels are striking, even given the obvious exceptional periods of the American Revolutionary War and the Napoleonic Wars, the fifth and sixth phases of the Second Hundred Years' War between Great Britain and France.

TABLE E-1

PERIODS OF EXPANSION AND CONTRACTION
IN THE ECONOMY OF THE UNITED STATES, 1665–1853

DATES OF PEAKS AND TROUGHS BY CALENDAR YEARS		LENGTH OF CYCLE IN YEARS	
Trough	Peak	Trough to Trough	Peak to Peak
	1668		
1670	1671		3
1673	1674	3	3
1679	1681	6	7
1684	1685	5	4
1688	1691	4	6
1693	1694	5	3
1695	1696	2	2
1698	1699	3	3
1700	1701	2	2
1703	1704	3	3
1705	1706	2	2
1708	1709	3	3
1712	1713	4	4
1714	1715	2	2
1716	1717	2	2
1718	1719	2	2
1721	1725	3	6
1726	1727	5	2
1734	1735	8	8
1736	1738	2	3
1739	1741	3	3
1745	1752	6	11
1756	1759	11	7
1761	1762	5	3
1764	1766	3	4
1768	1770	4	4

DATES OF PEAKS AND TROUGHS BY CALENDAR YEARS		LENGTH OF CYCLE IN YEARS	
Trough	Peak	Trough to Trough	Peak to Peak
1771	1772	3	2
1775	1778	4	6
1779	1780	4	2
1781	1782	2	2
1789	1796	8	14
1799	1801	10	5
1802	1806	3	5
1807	1808	5	2
1810	1814	3	6
1821	1822	11	8
1824	1827	3	5
1833	1837	9	10
1843	1847	10	10
1849	1850	6	3
1851	1853	2	3

NOTES AND SOURCES: The periods are identified in Table A-1, Column 6. Compare Figure 1. Sometimes they modify the beginning or the ending of the periods set out in a similar discussion in McCusker and Menard, *The Economy of British America, 1607–1789* (2d ed., 1991), 62–63, Table 3.4. Some of the data have been reinterpreted here.

BIBLIOGRAPHY

ELECTRONIC RESOURCES

Davies, Roy. 'Money—Past, Present & Future—Sources of Information on Monetary History, Contemporary Developments, and the Prospects for Electronic Money.' http://www.ex.ac.uk/~RDavies/arian/money.html (November 17, 2000).

EH.Net. 'How Much Is That?' http://www.eh.net (March 15, 2000).

Federal Reserve Bank of Philadelphia. http://www.phil.frb.org (November 17, 2000).

Great Britain. Office for National Statistics. http://www.statistics.gov.uk. (July 4, 2001).

Michener, Ronald W. 'The Leslie Brock Center for the Study of Colonial Currency.' http://www.virginia.edu/~econ/brock.html; http://www.virginia.edu/~econ/brock.html (November 17, 2000).

National Bureau of Economic Research. http://www.nber.org/cycles.html (November 17, 2000).

United States. Department of Labor. Bureau of Labor Statistics. http://stats.bls.gov (January 27, 2000); http://stats.bls.gov/cpi.nro.htm (July 4, 2001).

PRIMARY DOCUMENTS

Belgium
BRUSSELS
Algemeen Rijksarchief / Archives Générales du Royaume
Archives de la Secrétairerie d'État et de Guerre
Archives de la Secrétairerie Autrichienne d'État et de Guerre, 1717–1794
Archives de la Secrétairerie d'État
Affaires Économiques, 1725–1794
Commerce avec l'Amérique, 1783–1791 (*SEG* nos. 2162–2165)

Great Britain
LONDON
British Library
Department of Rare Books and Music

*London School of Economics and Political Science, British Library of
Political and Economic Science, University of London*
Manuscript Department
G. A. Falla. 'A Catalogue of the Papers of William Henry
Beveridge, 1st Baron Beveridge.' Unpublished typescript,
1981
Beveridge Wages and Price Collection

Public Record Office (PRO)
Colonial Office Records
CO 1 Colonial Papers, General Series, 1574–1757
CO 5 America and West Indies, Original Correspondence,
1606–1822
Exchequer and Audit Department Records
AO 12 Loyalist Claims Commission, Series I: Commission
Records, 1776–1831
AO 13 Loyalist Claims Commission, Series II: Original
Claims, 1780–1835
State Paper Office Records
SP 18 State Papers Domestic, Interregnum, Council of State,
Orders and Papers, 1649–1660

EDINBURGH, SCOTLAND
National Library of Scotland
Manuscript Department
MSS. 5027–5046, Charters 3887, 4006, Charles Steuart Pa-
pers, 1758–1797

Netherlands
AMSTERDAM
Internationaal Instituut voor Sociale Geschiedenis
Nederlandsch Economisch-Historisch Archief
Collectie Commerciële Couranten, 1580–1870
Collectie N. W. Posthumus, 1919–1949
Economisch-Historische Bibliotheek

United States of America
DISTRICT OF COLUMBIA
Washington
Library of Congress
Division of Rare Books and Special Collections

MASSACHUSETTS
Boston
Baker Library, Graduate School of Business Administration, Harvard University
Manuscripts and Archives Department
Records of the International Scientific Committee on Price History, 1928–1939
Massachusetts State Archives Facility, Columbia Point
Archives of the Commonwealth of Massachusetts
Massachusetts Judicial Archives
Middlesex County Probate Records, 1648–1871
Massachusetts Historical Society
Daniel Parker Papers, 1777–1812
Cambridge
Harvard University Library, Harvard University
Harvard College Library
Houghton Library
Jared Sparks Manuscripts
V. American Papers, 1493–1814

NEW YORK
Ithaca
Albert R. Mann Library, Cornell University
Frank Ashmore Pearson Papers
New York City
New York Public Library
Manuscript and Archives Division
George Chalmers Papers, 1606–1812
Maryland, 1619–1812
Transcripts of the Manuscript Books and Papers of the Commission of Enquiry into the Losses and Services of the American Loyalists, 1783–1790

PENNSYLVANIA
Philadelphia
Department of Economics, Library Wharton School of Finance and Commerce, University of Pennsylvania
Papers of the 'I[ndustrial] R[esearch] D[epartment], Wholesale Prices'

PRINTED RESOURCES

An Account of the True Market-Price of Wheat, and Malt, at Windsor, for 100 Years. Begun & Published by Wm. Fleetwood B[isho]p of Ely from 1646 to 1706. And Since Continued in the Same Manner. London, [1745?].

Adams, Donald R., Jr. 'One Hundred Years of Prices and Wages: Maryland, 1750–1850,' *Working Papers from the Regional Economic History Research Center,* 5 (No. 4, 1985): 90–129.

——. 'Prices and Wages.' In *Encyclopedia of American Economic History: Studies of the Principal Movements and Ideas,* ed. [Patrick] Glenn Porter, 1:229–46. New York: Charles Scribner's Sons, 1980.

——. 'Prices and Wages in Maryland, 1750–1850,' *Journal of Economic History,* 48 (September 1986): 625–45.

——. 'Wage Rates in the Early National Period: Philadelphia, 1785–1830,' *Journal of Economic History,* 26 (September 1968): 404–26.

America's Copper Coinage, 1783–1857. [Ed. Richard G. Doty]. Coinage of the Americas Conference, No. 1. New York: American Numismatic Society, 1984.

America's Silver Dollars. [Ed. John M. Kleeberg]. Coinage of the Americas Conference, No. 9. New York: American Numismatic Society, 1985.

The American Business Cycle: Continuity and Change. Ed. Robert J. Gordon. National Bureau of Economic Research, *Studies in Business Cycles,* Vol. 25. Chicago: University of Chicago Press, 1986.

Anderson, Terry Lee. *The Economic Growth of Seventeenth Century New England: A Measurement of Regional Income.* Ph.D. diss., University of Washington, 1972; New York: Arno Press, 1975.

——. 'Wealth Estimates for the New England Colonies, 1650–1709,' *Explorations in Economic History,* 12 (April 1975): 151–76.

Ashton, T[homas] S. *Economic Fluctuations in England, 1700–1800.* Oxford: Clarendon Press, 1959.

Backus, David K., and Patrick J. Kehoe. 'International Evidence on the Historical Properties of Business Cycles,' *American Economic Review,* 82 (September 1992): 864–88.

[Beelen-Bertholff, Fréderick Eugène François, baron de]. *Die Berichte des ersten Agenten Österreichs in den Vereinigten Staaten von Amerika, Baron de Beelen-Bertholff an Die Regierung der Österreichischen Niederlande in Brüssel, 1784–1789.* Ed. Hanns Schlitter. Fontes Rerum Austriacarum /Œsterreichische Geschichts-Quellen, Zwiete Abtheilung: Diplomataria et Acta, 45. Band, Zweite Hälfte. Vienna: F. Tempsky, 1891.

Berry, Thomas Senior. *Western Prices before 1861: A Study of the Cincinnati Market*, Harvard Economic Studies, Vol. 74. Cambridge Harvard University Press, 1943.

Beveridge, William [Henry]. *Prices and Wages in England from the Twelfth to the Nineteenth Century.* London: Longmans, Green and Co., 1939.

Bezanson, Anne, Blanch Daley, Marjorie C. Denison, and Miriam Hussey. *Prices and Inflation during the American Revolution: Pennsylvania, 1770–1790.* Philadelphia: University of Pennsylvania Press, 1951.

Bezanson, Anne, Robert D. Gray, and Miriam Hussey. *Prices in Colonial Pennsylvania.* Philadelphia: University of Pennsylvania Press, 1935.

——. *Wholesale Prices in Colonial Pennsylvania, 1784–1861.* 2 vols. Philadelphia: University of Pennsylvania Press, 1936–37.

Boorsma, Peter, and Joost van Genabeek. *Commercial and Financial Serial Publications of the Netherlands Economic History Archives: Commodity Price Currents, Foreign Exchange Rate Currents, Stock Exchange Rate Currents and Auction Lists, 1580–1870.* Nederlandsch Economisch-Historisch Archief, Inventarisatie Bijzondere Collecties 4. Amsterdam: Nederlandsch Economisch-Historisch Archief, 1991.

Boorsma, Peter, and Jan Lucassen. *Gids van de Collecties van het Nederlandsch Economisch-Historisch Archief te Amsterdam.* Nederlandsch Economisch-Historisch Archief, Ser. 5, No. 6. Amsterdam: Nederlandsch Economisch-Historisch Archief, 1992.

Bootle, Roger P. *The Death of Inflation: Surviving & Thriving in the Zero Era.* 2nd ed. London: Nicholas Brealey, 1997.

Bordo, Michael D., and Anna J. Schwartz. 'Money and Prices in the 19th Century: Was Thomas Tooke Right?' *Explorations in Economic History*, 18 (April 1981): 97–127.

Boskin, Michael J., et al. 'Consumer Prices, the Consumer Price Index, and the Cost of Living,' *Journal of Economic Perspectives*, 12 (Winter 1998): 3–26.

Brock, Leslie V. *The Currency of the American Colonies, 1700–1764: A Study in Colonial Finance and Imperial Relations.* Ph.D. diss., University of Michigan, 1941; New York: Arno Press, 1975.

Bullock, Charles J. *The Finances of the United States from 1775 to 1789, with Especial Reference to the Budget.* Bulletin of the University of Wisconsin, Economics, Political Science, and History Series, Vol. 1, No. 2. Madison: University of Wisconsin, 1895.

Burns, Arthur F., and Wesley C. Mitchell. *Measuring Business Cycles*, National Bureau of Economic Research, Studies in Business Cycles, Vol. 2. New York: National Bureau of Economic Research, 1946.

'Business Cycle Expansions and Contractions in the United States,' *Business Conditions Digest*, 30 (January 1990): 104.

Business Cycles and Depressions: An Encyclopedia. Ed. David Glasner. New York: Garland Publishing, 1997.

Cajori, Florian. *A History of Mathematical Notations*. 2 vols. Chicago: Open Court Publishing Company, [1928–29].

Calbetó de Grau, Gabriel. *Compendio de las Piezas de Ocho Reales*. 2 vols. San Juan, Puerto Rico: Ediciones Juan Ponce de Leon, 1970.

Calomiris, Charles W. 'The Depreciation of the Continental: A Reply,' *Journal of Economic History*, 48 (September 1988), 693–98.

Calomiris, Charles W. 'Institutional Failure, Monetary Scarcity, and the Depreciation of the Continental,' *Journal of Economic History*, 48 (March 1988): 47–68.

Carli, Giovanni Rinaldo. *Delle Monete e dell'Instituzione delle Zecche d'Italia, dell'Antico, e Presente Sistema d'Esse e del Loro Intrinseco Valore, e Rapporto con la Presente Moneta dalla Decadenza dell'Impero sino Secolo XVII*. 3 parts in 4 vols. Mantua: n.p., 1754; Pisa: Giovan Paolo Giovannelli, e Compagni, 1757; and Lucca, Italy: Jacopo Giusti, 1760.

Chalmers, Robert. *A History of Currency in the British Colonies* (London: Her Majesty's Stationer's Office [1893]).

Chang, Roberto. 'Dollarization: A Scorecard,' *Economic Review—Federal Reserve Bank of Atlanta*, [85] (Third Quarter, 2000): 1–11.

Chaplin, Joseph. *The Trader's Best Companion: Containing Various Arithmetical Rules . . . Applied to the Federal Currency. . . .* Newburyport, Mass.: William Barrett, 1795.

Chaudhuri, K[irti]. N. *The Trading World of Asia and the English East India Company, 1660–1760*. Cambridge: Cambridge University Press, 1978.

Clark, G[eorge] N. 'The Occasion of Fleetwood's "Chronicon Preciosum",' *English Historical Review*, 60 (October 1936): 686–90.

[Cochran, Thomas C.]. 'A Survey of Concepts and Viewpoints in the Social Sciences.' In *The Social Sciences in Historical Study: A Report of the Committee on Historiography*, [ed. Hugh G. J. Aitken], Social Science Research Council, Bulletin 64. New York: Social Science Research Council, 1965, 34–85.

Cockroft, Grace Amelia. *The Public Life of George Chalmers*. Columbia University, Studies in History, Economics and Public Law, No. 454. New York: Columbia University Press, 1939.

Cole, Arthur Harrison. *Wholesale Commodity Prices in the United States, 1700–1861.* 2 vols. Cambridge: Harvard University Press, 1938.

Cole, Arthur H., and Ruth Crandall. 'The International Scientific Committee on Price History,' *Journal of Economic History*, 24 (September 1964): 381–88.

Connecticut. Laws and Statutes. *At a General Assembly of the Governor and Company of the State of Connecticut, Holden at Hartford, on the Second Thursday of October, A.D. 1780. An Act to Ascertain the Current Value of Continental Bills of Credit in Spanish Milled Dollars in This State, and of Contracts Made For the Payment Thereof, in the Several Periods of Its Depreciation.* Hartford: Hudson and Goodwin, 1780.

Consumption and the World of Goods. Ed. John Brewer and Roy Potter. London and New York: Routledge, 1993.

Cooper, James C., and Karl Borden. 'Public Representation of Historical Prices: An Interdisciplinary Opportunity,' *Essays in Economic and Business History: The Journal of the Economic and Business Historical Society*, 14 (1996): 465–85.

Coquelin, Ch[arles], and [Gilbert Urbain] Guillaumin. *Dictionnaire de l'économie politique.* 3d ed. 2 vols. Paris: Guillaumin & Cie., 1864.

Craven, B. M., and R. Gausden. 'How Best to Measure Inflation? The UK and Europe,' *The Royal Bank of Scotland Review*, No. 170 (June 1991): 26–37.

Crowe, Walter R. *Index Numbers: Theory and Application.* London: Macdonald & Evans Ltd., 1965.

David, Paul A. *Real Income and Economic Welfare Growth in the Early Republic or, Another Try at Getting the American Story Straight.* Discussion Papers in Economic and Social History, No. 5. Oxford: Clarendon Press, 1996.

David, Paul A., and Peter Solar. 'A Bicentenary Contribution to the History of the Cost of Living in America,' *Research in Economic History*, 2 (1977): 1–80.

Davis, Ralph. *The Industrial Revolution and British Overseas Trade.* Leicester, England: Leicester University Press, 1979.

Davisson, William I. 'Essex County Price Trends: Money and Markets in Seventeenth Century Massachusetts.' *Essex Institute Historical Collections*, 103 (April 1967): 141–85.

Deane, Phyllis, and W[illiam] A. Cole. *British Economic Growth, 1688–1959: Trends and Structure.* 2d ed. Cambridge: Cambridge University Press, 1969.

De Roover, Raymond [A.] *The Medici Bank: Its Organization, Management, Operations, and Decline.* New York: New York University Press, 1948.

Desbarats, Catherine M. 'Colonial Government Finances in New France, 1700–1750.' Ph.D. diss., McGill University, 1993.

Desloges, Yvon. *A Tenant's Town: Quèbec in the Eighteenth Century.* [Trans. Department of the Secretary of State.] [Ottawa: Environment Canada, Parks Service, 1991].

Diewert, W[alter] E. 'Index Numbers,' in *The New Palgrave: A Dictionary of Economics.* Ed. John Eatwell, Murray Milgate, and Peter Newman, 2:767–80. London: Macmillan Ltd., 1987.

Dobson, C. R. *Masters and Journeymen: A Prehistory of Industrial Relations, 1717–1800.* London: Croom Helm, and Totowa, N.J.: Rowman and Littlefield, [1980].

Dowland, John. *Booke of Songes or Ayres.* 3 vols. London: Thomas Adams et al., 1597–1613.

[Dupré de Saint-Maur, Nicolas François]. *Recherches sur la valeur des monnoies, et sur le prix des grains, avant et après le Concile de Francfort [1409].* Paris: Nyon, Didot and Saugrain, 1762.

[Dutot, Charles de Ferrare]. *Réflexions politiques sur les finances et le commerce. Où l'on examine quelles ont été sur les revenus, les denrées, le change étranger, & conséquemment sur notre commerce, les influences des augmentations et les diminutions des valeurs numéraires des monnoyes.* 2 vols. The Hague, Netherland: V[aillant] and N[icolas] Prevost, 1738.

Eichhorn, Wolfgang. *Measurement in Economics: Theory and Application of Economic Indices.* Heidelberg, Germany: Physica-Verlag, 1988.

Encyclopedia of American Economic History: Studies of the Principal Movements and Ideas. Ed. [Patrick] Glenn Porter. 3 vols. New York: Charles Scribner's Sons, 1980.

Essays on the Price History of Eighteenth-Century Latin America. Ed. Lyman L. Johnson and Enrique Tandeter. Albuquerque, N.M.: University of New Mexico Press, [1990].

Faulkner, Harold Underwood. *American Economic History.* Ed. Harry N. Scheiber and Harold G. Vatter. 9th ed., rev. New York: Harper & Row, [1976].

The Federal, or New Ready Reckoner . . . Chestnut Hill [Philadelphia]: Samuel Sower, 1793.

Feinstein, Charles [H.] *Conjectures and Contrivances: Economic Growth and the Standard of Living in Britain during the Industrial Revolution.* Discussion Papers in Economic and Social History, No. 9. [Oxford]: University of Oxford, [1996].

Ferguson, E[lmer] James. *The Power of the Purse: A History of American Public Finance, 1776–1790.* Chapel Hill: University of North Carolina Press, 1961.

Fisher, Douglas. *The Industrial Revolution: A Macroeconomic Interpretation.* London: Macmillan, 1992.

Fisher, Franklin M., and Karl Shell. 'Taste and Quality Change in the Pure Theory of the True Cost-of-Living Index.' In *Value, Capital, and Growth: Papers in Honour of Sir John Hicks,* ed. J[ames] N. Wolfe, 97–139. Edinburgh: Edinburgh University Press, 1967.

Fisher, Irving. *The Making of Index Numbers: A Study of Their Varieties, Tests, and Reliability.* 3d ed., rev. Boston: Houghton Mifflin Co., 1927.

Fisher, Irving, and Harry G. Brown. *The Purchasing Power of Money: Its Determination and Relation to Credit, Interest, and Crises.* Rev. ed. New York: Macmillan, 1922.

Fisher, Willard C. 'The Tabular Standard in Massachusetts History.' *Quarterly Journal of Economics,* 27 (May 1913): 417–51.

Fite, Gilbert C., and Jim E. Reese. *An Economic History of the United States.* 3d ed. Boston: Houghton Mifflin Co., 1973.

[Fitzpatrick, F. A.] *Wholesale Price Index: Principles and Procedures. Studies in Official Statistics,* No. 32. London: Her Majesty's Stationer's Office, [1980].

Fleetwood, [William]. *Chronicon Preciosum: or, An Account of English Gold and Silver Money, the Price of Corn, and Other Commodities, . . . &c. in England, for Six Hundred Years Last Past.* Rev. ed. London: T[homas] Osborne, 1745.

Flinn, M[ichael] W. 'Trends in Real Wages, 1750–1850,' *Economic History Review,* 2d Ser., 27 (August 1974): 399–413.

Floud, Roderick. *An Introduction to Quantitative Methods for Historians.* 2d ed. London: Methuen, [1979].

Fogel, Robert William. *Without Consent or Contract: The Rise and Fall of American Slavery* (New York: W. W. Norton & Company, 1989).

Fourastié, Jacqueline. *Les formules d'indices de prix: Calculs numériques et commentaires théoriques.* Paris: Librairie Armand Colin, 1966.

Fowler, R[onald] F. *Some Problems of Index Number Construction.* Studies in Official Statistics, Research Series, No. 3. London: Her Majesty's Stationer's Office, 1970.

Franklin, Benjamin. *A Modest Inquiry into the Nature and Necessity of a Paper-Currency.* Philadelphia: New Printing Office, 1729.

——. *The Papers of Benjamin Franklin*, ed. Leonard W. Labaree et al. New Haven: Yale University Press, 1959–.

Freeman, Samuel. *A Valuable Assistant to Every Man: or, the American Clerk's Magazine.* 2d ed. Boston: I[saiah] Thomas and E[benezer] T. Andrews, 1795.

Gallman, Robert E. 'Comment,' *Journal of Economic History*, 39 (March 1979): 311–12.

Gentlemen Prefer Blondes [New York]: Columbia Records, [1950].

Georgia, Laws and Statutes. *An Act to Ascertain the Various Periods of Depreciation, for the Government and Regulation of All and Every Person or Persons Whom the Same May Concern.* [Savannah: James Johnston, 1783].

Gilboy, Elizabeth W. 'The Cost of Living and Real Wages in Eighteenth Century England,' *Review of Economic Statistics*, 18 (1936): 134–43.

Gibson, A[lex] J. S., and T[homas] C[hristopher] Smout. *Prices, Food and Wages in Scotland, 1550–1780.* [Cambridge]: Cambridge University Press, 1995.

Gordon, Donald F. 'Value, Labor Theory of.' In *International Encyclopedia of the Social Sciences*, ed. David L. Sills, 16:279–83. [New York:] Macmillan & The Free Press, [1968].

Great Britain. Laws and Statutes. *The General Public Acts . . .* London: Her Majesty's Stationer's Office, 1831–.

——. *The Statutes at Large . . . of Great Britain.* Ed. Danby Pickering. 46 vols. Cambridge: Cambridge University Press, 1762–1807.

Great Britain. Office for National Statistics. *Annual Abstract of Statistics.* London: Her Majesty's Stationer's Office, 1853–. Title and issuing office varies.

——. *Economic Trends.* (Monthly since 1953). Title and issuing office varies.

——. *Labour Market Trends* (monthly since 1893). Title and issuing office varies.

——. *Monthly Digest of Statistics* (monthly since 1980). Title and issuing office varies.

——. *Retail Prices Index: A Brief Guide to the RPI.* London: Her Majesty's Stationer's Office, 1996.

——. Retail Prices, 1914–1990 (London: Her Majesty's Stationer's Office, 1991).

Grierson, Philip. 'Money and Coinage under Charlemagne.' In *Karl der Grosse: lebenswerk und Nachleben.* Ed. Wolfgang Braunfels et al., 3:501–36. 3d ed. Düsseldorf: L. Schwann, [1967–68].

Gunnarsson, Gìsli. 'A Study in the Historiography of Prices,' *Economy and History*, 19 (1976): 124–41.

Gwyn, Julian. 'British Government Spending and the North American Colonies, 1740–1775,' *Journal of Imperial and Commonwealth History*, 8 (January 1980): 74–84.

Haines, Michael R. 'A State and Local Consumer Price Index for the United States in 1890,' *Historical Methods: A Journal of Quantitative and Interdisciplinary History*, 22 (Summer 1989): 97–105.

Hall, Thomas E. *Business Cycles: The Nature and Causes of Economic Fluctuations.* New York: Praeger Publishers, 1990.

Hamilton, Alexander. *The Papers of Alexander Hamilton.* Ed. Harold C. Syrett et al. 26 vols. New York: Columbia University Press, 1961–79.

Hamilton, Earl J. 'Prices, Wages, and the Industrial Revolution.' In *Studies in Economics and Industrial Relations*, by Wesley C. Mitchell et al., 99–112. Philadelphia: University of Pennsylvania Press, 1941.

——. 'Use and Misuse of Price History.' In *The Tasks of Economic History: Papers Presented at the Fourth Annual Meeting of the Economic History Association — A Supplemental Issue of the Journal of Economic History*, [Supplement 4], 47–60. New York: Economic History Association, 1944.

——. *War and Prices in Spain, 1651–1800.* Harvard Economic Studies, Vol. 81. Cambridge, Mass.: Harvard University Press, 1947.

Hardy, Stephen G. 'Trade and Economic Growth in the Eighteenth-Century Chesapeake.' Ph.D. diss., University of Maryland, 1999.

Harris, P. M. G. 'Inflation and Deflation in Early America, 1634–1860: Patterns of Change in the British-American Economy,' *Social Science History*, 20 (Winter 1996): 469–505.

Heiss, Aloïss. *Descripción general de las monedas hispano-cristianas desde la invasión de los Árabes.* 3 vols. Madrid: R. N. Milagro, 1865–69.

Hewitt, John. *A Treatise upon Money, Coins, and Exchange . . .* 1st ed. London: T[homas] Cox, 1740.

Hiden, Mrs. Philip Wallace [Martha]. 'The Money of Colonial Virginia,' *Virginia Magazine of History and Biography*, 60 (January 1943): 36–54.

Holcomb, Brent H. *South Carolina Deed Abstracts* [1773–1788]. 3 vols. [Columbia, S.C.: SCMAR, 1993–96].

Hughes, Jonathan [R. T.] *American Economic History*. 3d. ed. Glenview, Ill.: Scott, Foresman and Co., 1990.

——. *Fluctuations in Trade, Industry, and Finance*. Oxford: Clarendon Press, 1960.

Hughes, J[onathan] R. T., and Nathan Rosenberg. 'The United States Business Cycle before 1860: Some Problems of Interpretation,' *Economic History Review*, 2d. ser. 15 (December 1963): 476–93.

Hume, David. *Essays, Moral, Political, and Literary*. Ed. Eugene F. Miller. Rev. ed. Indianapolis, Ind.: Liberty Classics, 1985.

——. *Political Discourses*. Edinburgh: A. Kincaid and A. Donaldson, 1752.

Hutchison, Terence [W.]. *Before Adam Smith: The Emergence of Political Economy, 1662–1776*. Oxford: Basil Blackwell, [1988].

Index Numbers of Wholesale Prices in the United States and Foreign Countries. United States, Department of Labor, Bureau of Labor Statistics, Bulletin No. 284. Washington, D.C.: Government Printing Office, 1921.

International Encyclopedia of the Social Sciences. Ed. David L. Sills and Robert K. Merton. 19 vols. [New York:] Macmillan & The Free Press, [1968–91].

International Monetary Conference, 1878, Paris. *Proceedings and Exhibits, Followed by the Report of the American Commission* . . . [U.S. Congress. 45th Cong., 3d session. Senate Executive Document, No. 58. Serial Set No. 1832]. Washington, D.C.: Government Printing Office, 1879.

International Monetary Fund. International Financial Statistics. (monthly since 1947).

Inventaires après-décès et ventes de meubles: Rapports à une histoire de la vie économique et quotidienne (XIVe–XIXe siècles). Ed. Micheline Baulant, Anton J. Schuurman, and Paul Servais. Actes du Séminaire Tenu dans le Cadre du 9ème Congrès International d'Histoire Économique de Berne. Louvain-la-Neuve, Belgium: Academia, 1988.

Jastram, Roy W. *The Golden Constant: The English and American Experience, 1560–1976*. New York: John Wiley & Sons, [1977].

——. *Silver: The Restless Metal*. New York: John Wiley & Sons, [1981].

Jefferson, Thomas. *The Papers of Thomas Jefferson.* Ed. Julian P. Boyd et al. Princeton: Princeton University Press, 1950–.

Jones, Alice Hanson. *American Colonial Wealth: Documents and Methods.* 2d ed. 3 vols. New York: Arno Press, 1978.

—. 'American Colonial Wealth: Documents and Methods for the American Middle Colonies, 1774,' *Economic Development and Cultural Change*, 18 (July 1970): 124–40.

Karl der Grosse: Lebenswerk und Nachleben. Ed. Wolfgang Braunfels et al. [3d ed.]. 5 vols. Düsseldorf, Ger.: L. Schwann, [1967–68].

Klein, Herbert S., and Stanley L. Engerman. 'Methods and Meanings in Price History.' In *Essays on the Price History of Eighteenth-Century Latin America*, ed. Lyman L. Johnson and Enrique Tandeter, 9–20. Albuquerque, N.M.: University of New Mexico Press, [1990].

Klingaman, David C. *Colonial Virginia's Coastwise and Grain Trade.* Ph.D. diss., University of Virginia, 1972; New York: Arno Press, 1975.

Krause, Chester L., and Clifford Mishler. *Standard Catalog of World Coins: Eighteenth Century, 1701–1800.* 2d ed. Isola, Wis.: Krause Publications, 1997.

Kravis, Irving B. 'Comparative Studies of National Incomes and Prices,' *Journal of Economic Literature*, 22 (March 1984): 1–39.

Kydland, Finn E., and Edward C. Prescott. 'Business Cycles: Real Facts and a Monetary Myth,' *Federal Reserve Bank of Minneapolis Quarterly Review*, 14 (Spring 1990): 3–18.

Lagerqvist, Lars O., and Ernst Nathorst-Böös. *Vad kostade det?: Priser och löner* från medeltid til våra dagar. [3d ed., rev.]. Stockholm: LTs Förlag, [1993].

Landes, David S. *The Wealth and Poverty of Nations: Why Some Are So Rich and Some So Poor.* New York: W. W. Norton & Co., [1998].

Landowners, Capitalists and Entrepreneurs: Essays for Sir John Habakkuk. Ed. F[rancis] M. L. Thompson. Oxford: Clarendon Press, 1994.

Lebergott, Stanley. *Manpower in Economic Growth: The American Record since 1800.* New York: McGraw-Hill, 1964.

—. 'Wage Trends, 1800–1900.' In *Trends in the American Economy in the Nineteenth Century*, ed. William N. Parker, 24: 449–99. National Bureau of Economic Research, Studies in Income and Wealth. Princeton: Princeton University Press, 1960.

Lee, Chauncey. *The American Accomptant; Being a Plain, Practical and Systematic Compendium of Federal Arithmetic. . . .* Lansingburgh [Troy], New York: William W. Wands, 1797.

Lindert, Peter H. 'Probates, Prices, and Preindustrial Living Standards.' In *Inventaires après-décès et ventes de meubles: Rapports à une histoire de la vie économique et quotidienne (XIVe-XIXe siècles)*, ed. Micheline Baulant, Anton J. Schuurman, and Paul Servais, Actes du Séminaire Tenu dans le Cadre du 9ème Congrès International d'Histoire Économique de Berne. Louvain-la-Neuve, Belgium: Academia, 1988, 171–80.

Lippincott, Joseph. *A Collection of Tables . . . Shewing the Value of Any Number of Pounds, Shillings and Pence in Dollars and Cents. . . .* Philadelphia: Benjamin Johnson, 1792.

Loschky, D[avid] [J.] 'Seven Centuries of Real Income per Wage Earner Reconsidered,' *Economica*, New Ser., 47 (November 1980): 459–65.

Lucas, Robert E., Jr. 'Understanding Business Cycles.' In *Stabilization of the Domestic and International Economy*, ed. Karl Brunner and Allan H. Meltzer, 5:7–29. Carnegie-Rochester Conference Series on Public Policy. Amsterdam: North-Holland Publishing Company, 1977.

Lydall, H[arold] F., and E[rnest] H. Phelps Brown. 'Seven Centuries of Real Income per Wage-Earner Reconsidered: A Note,' *Economica*, New Ser., 49 (May 1982): 201–5.

McCusker, John J. 'The Current Value of English Exports, 1697 to 1800.' *William and Mary Quarterly*, 3d. Ser., 28 (October 1971): 607–28.

——. *Essays in the Economic History of the Atlantic World*. London: Routledge, 1997.

——. 'How Much Is That in Real Money? A Historical Price Index for Use as a Deflator of Money Values in the Economy of the United States,' *Proceedings of the American Antiquarian Society*, 101 (October 1991): 297–373; repr. separately, 1992.

——. 'How Much Is That in Real Money? A Historical Price Index for Use as a Deflator of Money Values in the Economy of the United States: Addenda et Corrigenda.' *Proceedings of the American Antiquarian Society*, 106 (October 1996): 315–22.

——. Letter to the Editor. *Business History Review*, 68 (Summer 1994): 276–79.

——. *Money and Exchange in Europe and America, 1600–1775: A Handbook*. 2d. ed. Chapel Hill: University of North Carolina Press, [1992].

McCusker, John J., and Russell R. Menard. *The Economy of British Amer-*

ica, 1607–1789. 2d. ed. Chapel Hill: University of North Carolina Press, 1991.

McMaster, John Bach. *A History of the People of the United States from the Revolution to the Civil War.* 8 vols. New York: D. Appleton, 1883–1913.

Martin, David A. 'The Changing Role of Foreign Money in the United States, 1782–1857,' *Journal of Economic History,* 37 (December 1977): 1009–27.

Marty, Martin E. 'Another 120 Days, Another $18.75,' *The Christian Century,* 109, No. 25 (September 2, 1992): 791.

Marx, Karl. *Capital: A Critique of Political Economy.* Ed. Friedrich Engels. Trans. and ed. Samuel Moore and Edward [B.] Aveling, rev. Ernest Untermann. 3 vols. Chicago: Charles H. Kerr and Co., 1906–9.

Massachusetts (Colony). Laws and Statutes. *The Acts and Resolves, Public and Private, of the Province of the Massachusetts Bay.* [Ed. Abner Cheney Goodell et al.] 21 vols. Boston: Wright and Porter, 1869–1922.

Matthews, R[obert] C. O. *A Study in Trade-Cycle History: Economic Fluctuations in Great Britain, 1833–1842.* Cambridge: Cambridge University Press, 1954.

Meek, Ronald L. Smith. *Marx, & After: Ten Essays in the Development of Economic Thought.* London: Chapman & Hall, 1977.

——. *Studies in the Labour Theory of Value.* 2d. ed. London: Lawrence & Wishart, 1973.

Melville, Herman. *Moby-Dick or The Whale* (1851). Ed. Harrison Hayford, G[eorge] Thomas Tanselle, and Hershel Parker. The Writings of Herman Melville: The Northwestern-Newberry Edition, Vol. 6. Evanston and Chicago, Illinois: Northwestern University Press and The Newberry Library, 1988.

Michener, Ron[ald] [W.]. 'Backing Theories and the Currencies of Eighteenth-Century America.' *Journal of Economic History,* 48 (September 1988): 682–92.

Mitchell, Brian R. *British Historical Statistics.* Cambridge: Cambridge University Press, 1988.

Mitchell, Wesley C. 'The Making and Using of Index Numbers.' In *Index Numbers of Wholesale Prices in the United States and Foreign Countries.* United States, Department of Labor, Bureau of Labor Statistics, Bulletin No. 284. Washington, D.C.: Government Printing Office, 1921, 7–114.

Mitchell, Wesley C. et al. *Studies in Economics and Industrial Relations.* Philadelphia: University of Pennsylvania Press, 1941.

Moore, Geoffrey H. 'Business Cycles, Panics, and Depressions.' In *Encyclopedia of American Economic History: Studies of the Principal Movements and Ideas*, ed. [Patrick] Glenn Porter, 1:151–56. New York: Charles Scribner's Sons, 1980.

——. 'A Truism: Recession Slows Inflation,' *New York Times*, Sunday, November 18, 1979. [Business and Finance section.]

Moreno, Alvaro J. *El Signo $ de Pesos ¿Cuál es su Origen y qué Representa?* México: Edición Particular, 1965.

Morris, Richard B. ed. *Encyclopedia of American History*. Rev. ed. New York: Harper & Row, 1965.

Morris, Robert. *The Papers of Robert Morris, 1781–1784.* Ed. E[lmer] James Ferguson, et al. 9 vols. Pittsburgh: University of Pittsburgh Press, 1973–99.

Mossman, Philip L. *Money of the American Colonies and Confederation: A Numismatic, Economic and Historical Correlation.* Numismatic Studies No. 20. New York: American Numismatic Society, 1993.

Mudgett, Bruce D. *Index Numbers.* New York: John Wiley & Sons, 1951.

Munby, Lionel [M.] *How Much Is That Worth?* 1st ed. [Salisbury, England]: British Association for Local History, [1989].

Nevins, Alan. *The American States during and after the Revolution, 1775–1789.* New York: Macmillan, 1927.

New Hampshire. General Court. House of Representatives. *State of New-Hampshire. In the House of Representatives, July 3, 1781. The Committee to Form a Table Or Scale of Depreciation For This State, Reported As Their Opinion, That All Contracts Previous to the Last Day of January 1777, Shall Be Considered As Silver and Gold; and All Contracts For Paper Money From the Last Day of January 1777 to the Last Day of June 1781, to Be Computed in the Following Manner . . .* [Exeter, N.H.: Zechariah Fowle, 1781].

The New Palgrave: A Dictionary of Economics. Ed. John Eatwell, Murray Milgate, and Peter Newman, 4 vols. London: Macmillan Press Ltd., 1987.

Newman, Eric P. 'Circulation of Pre-U.S. Mint Coppers.' In *America's Copper Coinage, 1783–1857*, 101–16. New York: American Numismatic Society, 1984.

——. 'The Earliest Money Using the Dollar as an Official Unit of Value.' *The Numismatist*, 98 (November 1985): 2181–87.

——. *The Early Paper Money of America.* 3d ed. [Isola, Wis.: Krause Publications], 1990.

Niles' Weekly Register (Baltimore and Philadelphia, 1811–1849). Title varies.

Oldham, James C. 'The Origins of the Special Jury.' *University of Chicago Law Review*, 50 (Winter 1983): 137–221.

[Petty, William]. *A Treatise of Taxes & Contributions: Shewing the Nature and Measures of Crown-Lands.* . . . London: N[athaniel] Brooke, 1662.

Phelps Brown, [Ernest] Henry. 'Gregory King's Notebook and the Phelps Brown-Hopkins Price Index.' *Economic History Review*, 2d. Ser., 43 (February 1990): 99–103.

Phelps Brown, E[rnest] H., and Sheila V. Hopkins. 'Seven Centuries of the Prices of Consumables, compared with Builders' Wage-rates.' *Economica*, new ser., 23 (November 1956): 296–314.

——. *A Perspective of Wages and Prices.* London and New York: Methuen, 1981.

Phillips, Henry, Jr. *Historical Sketches of the Paper Currency of the American Colonies, prior to the Adoption of the Federal Constitution.* 2 vols. Roxbury, Mass.: W. Elliot Woodward, 1865.

Pike, Nicholas. *A New and Complete System of Arithmetic, Composed for the Use of the Citizens of the United States.* 1st ed. Newburyport, Mass.: John Mycall, 1788.

A Pocket Almanack for the Year 1751. Fitted to the Use of Pennsylvania, and All the Neighbouring Provinces. Philadelphia: B[enjamin] Franklin and D[avid] Hall, [1750].

Pollak, Robert A. *The Theory of the Cost-of-Living Index.* New York: Oxford University Press, 1989.

Pond, Shepard. 'The Spanish Dollar: The World's Most Famous Silver Coin.' *Bulletin of the Business Historical Society*, 15 (February 1941): 12–16.

Posthumus, N[icolaas] W. *Nederlandsche Prijsgeschiedenis*, 2 vols. Leiden: E. J. Brill, 1943–64.

I Prezzi in Europa del XIII Secolo a Oggi. Ed. Ruggiero Romano [Turin]: Guilio Einaudi, [1967].

Price Indexes and Quality Change: Studies in New Methods of Measurement. Ed. Zvi Griliches. Cambridge: Harvard University Press, 1971.

'The Provincial Currency of Maryland.' *[Fisher's] National Magazine and Industrial Record*, 2 (January 1846): 683–701.

Raguet, Condy. *A Treatise on Currency and Banking*, 2d. ed. Philadelphia: Grigg and Elliot, 1840.

Ramsay, David. *The History of South-Carolina, from Its First Settlement in 1679, to the Year 1808.* 2 vols. Charleston, S.C.: The Author, 1809.

Reitlinger, Gerald. *The Economics of Taste.* 3 vols. London: Barrie and Rockliff, 1961–70.

Rolnik, Arthur J., Bruce D. Smith, and Warren E. Weber. 'The Origins of the Monetary Union in the United States.' In *Varieties of Monetary Reforms: Lessons and Experiences on the Road to Monetary Union*, ed. Pierre L. Siklos, 323–49. Boston: Kluwer Academic Publishers, [1994].

Romer, Christina D. 'The Prewar Business Cycle Reconsidered: New Estimates of Gross National Product, 1869–1908.' *Journal of Political Economy*, 98 (February 1989): 1–39.

Rostow, W[alt] W. *The World Economy: History & Prospect.* Austin: University of Texas Press, [1978].

Rostow, W[alt] W., and Michael Kennedy. 'A Simple Model of the Kondratieff Cycle.' *Research in Economic History*, 4 (1979): 1–36.

Rothenberg, Winifred B[arr]. 'The Emergence of a Capital Market in Rural Massachusetts, 1730–1838.' *Journal of Economy History*, 45 (December 1985): 781–808.

Rothenberg, Winifred Barr. *From Market-Places to a Market Economy: The Transformation of Rural Massachusetts, 1750–1850.* Chicago: University of Chicago Press, 1992.

——. 'A Price Index for Rural Massachusetts, 1750–1855.' *Journal of Economic History*, 39 (December 1979): 975–1001.

——. Review of *How Much Is That in Real Money? A Historical Price Index for Use as a Deflator of Money Values in the Economy of the United States*, by John J. McCusker. *Business History Review*, 67 (Autumn 1993): 462–65.

Ruist, Erik, Ethel D. Hoover, and Philip J. McCarthy. 'Index Numbers.' In *International Encyclopedia of the Social Sciences*, ed. David L. Sills, 7:154–69. [New York:] Macmillan & The Free Press, [1968].

Scale of Depreciation, Agreeable to An Act of the Commonwealth of Massachusetts, Passed September 29, 1780 to be Observed as a Rule for Settling the Rate of Depreciation on All Contracts, Public and Private, for the Payment of Monies Made on Or Since the First Day of January, 1777. [Boston]: T. & J. Fleet, [1781].

Scale of Depreciation, Agreeable to An Act of the (Now) Commonwealth of Massachusetts, Passed September 29, 1780. [Boston, 1781].

Samuelson, Paul A., and William D. Nordhaus. *Economics.* 12th ed. New York: McGraw-Hill, 1985.

Schilke, Oscar G., and Raphael E. Solomon. *America's Foreign Coins: An Illustrated Standard Catalogue with Valuations of Foreign Coins with Legal Tender Status in the United States, 1793–1857.* New York: Coin and Currency Institute, 1964.

Schneider, Jürgen, et al. *Währungen der Welt.* 14 parts in 11 vols. *Beiträge zur Wirtschafts- und Sozialgeschichte*, Nos. 44–50, 57, 59, 61. Stuttgart: Franz Steiner, 1991–96.

Schumpeter, Joseph A. *History of Economic Analysis.* Ed. [Romaine] Elizabeth Boody Schumpeter. New York: Oxford University Press, [1954].

Schumpeter, [Romaine] Elizabeth Boody. 'English Prices and Public Finance, 1660–1822.' *Review of Economic Statistics*, 20 (1938): 21–37.

Scott, William Robert. *The Constitution and Finance of English, Scottish, and Irish Joint-Stock Companies to 1720.* 3 vols. Cambridge: Cambridge University Press, 1911.

Smith, Adam. *An Inquiry into the Nature and Causes of the Wealth of Nations* (1776). Ed. R[oy] H. Campbell, A[ndrew] S. Skinner, and W[illiam] B. Todd. 2 vols. Oxford: Clarendon Press, 1976.

Smith, Billy G. '"The Best Poor Man's Country": Living Standards of the "Lower Sort" in Late Eighteenth-Century Philadelphia.' *Working Papers from the Regional Economic History Research Center*, 2 (No. 4, 1979): 1–70.

——. *The 'Lower Sort': Philadelphia's Laboring People, 1750–1800.* Ithaca, New York: Cornell University Press, [1990].

Smith, S[imon] D. 'The Market for Manufactures in the Thirteen Continental Colonies, 1698–1776.' *Economic History Review*, 2d ser. 60 (November 1998): 676–708.

——. 'Prices and the Value of English Exports in the Eighteenth Century: Evidence from the North American Colonial Trade.' *Economic History Review*, 2d ser. 68 (August 1995): 575–90.

Snelling, Thomas. *A View of the Coins at This Time Current Throughout Europe.* London: T[homas] Snelling, 1766.

The Social Sciences in Historical Study: A Report of the Committee on Historiography [Ed. Hugh G. J. Aitken]. Social Science Research Council Bulletin 64. New York: Social Science Research Council, 1965.

Solomon, Raphael E. 'Foreign Specie Coins in the American Colonies.' In *Studies on Money in Early America*, ed. Eric P. Newman and Richard G. Doty, 25–42. New York: American Numismatic Society, 1976.

South Carolina. Commissioners for Ascertaining the Progressive Depreciation of the Paper Currency. *An Accurate Table, Ascertaining the Progressive Depreciation of the Paper-Currency, in the Province of South-Carolina, during the Late Usurpation.* . . . Charleston, S.C.: John Wells, Jr., 1781.

South Carolina. Laws and Statutes. *The Statutes at Large of South Carolina*. Ed. Thomas Cooper and David J. McCord. 10 vols. Columbia, S.C.: A. S. Johnston, 1836–41.

Stabilization of the Domestic and International Economy. Ed. Karl Brunner and Allan H. Meltzer, Carnegie-Rochester Conference Series on Public Policy, Vol. 5. Amsterdam: North-Holland Publishing Company, 1977.

Stephenson, Neal. *Snow Crash*. New York: Bantam Books, 1992.

Studies on Money in Early America. Ed. Eric P. Newman and Richard G. Doty. New York: American Numismatic Society, 1976.

Sumner, W[illiam] G. 'The Spanish Dollar and the Colonial Shilling.' *American Historical Review*, 3 (July 1898): 607–19.

A Table Shewing the Value of Old Tenor Bills, in Lawful Money [Boston: Samuel Kneeland and Timothy Green (?), 1750].

The Tasks of Economic History: Papers Presented at the Fourth Annual Meeting of the Economic History Association — A Supplemental Issue of the Journal of Economic History, [Supplement 4]. New York, 1944.

Taylor, George Rogers. 'Wholesale Commodity Prices at Charleston, South Carolina, [1732–1861].' *Journal of Economic and Business History*, 4 (February and August 1932): 356–77, 848–[76].

Temin, Peter. 'Labour Scarcity and Capital Markets in America.' In *Landowners, Capitalists and Entrepreneurs: Essays for Sir John Habakkuk*, ed. F[rancis] M. L. Thompson, 257–73. Oxford: Clarendon Press, 1994.

Thomas, Lloyd B., Jr. 'Survey Measures of Expected U.S. Inflation.' *Journal of Economic Perspectives*, 13 (Fall 1999): 125–44.

Tobin, James. 'Fisher, Irving.' In *The New Palgrave: A Dictionary of Eco-*

nomics, ed. John Eatwell, Murray Milgate, and Peter Newman, 2:369–76. London: Macmillan, 1987.

Trends in the American Economy in the Nineteenth Century, ed. William N. Parker, National Bureau of Economic Research, Studies in Income and Wealth, Vol. 24. Princeton: Princeton University Press, 1960.

Turvey, Ralph. *Consumer Price Indexes: An ILO Manual*. Geneva, Switzerland: International Labour Office, 1989.

Ulmer, Melville J. *The Economic Theory of Cost of Living Index Numbers*. New York: Columbia University Press, 1949.

[United States. Congress]. *American State Papers: Documents, Legislative and Executive, of the Congress of the United States*. 38 vols. Washington, D.C.: Gales and Seaton, 1832–61.

United States. Congress. Joint Economic Committee. *Study of Employment, Growth, and Price Levels: Hearings before the Joint Economic Committee, Congress of the United States . . . April 7, 8, 9, and 10, 1959*. 86th Congress, 2d Session, 10 parts in 13 vols. Washington, D.C.: Government Printing Office, 1959–60.

United States. Congress. Senate Committee on Finance. *Wholesale Prices, Wages, and Transportation: Report by Mr. [Nelson W.] Aldrich, from the Committee on Finance, March 3, 1893*. 52d Congress, 2d Session, Senate Report No. 1394 [Serial Set No. 3074 (4 parts)]. Washington, D.C.: United States Government Printing Office, 1893.

United States. Continental Congress. *Journals of the Continental Congress, 1774–1789*. Ed. Worthington Chauncey Ford, et al. 34 vols. Washington, D.C.: Government Printing Office, 1904–37.

United States. Department of Commerce. Bureau of the Census. *Historical Statistics of the United States, Colonial Times to 1970*. [3d ed.] 2 vols. Washington, D.C.: United States Government Printing Office, 1975.

——. *Statistical Abstract of the United States*. Washington, D.C.: Government Printing Office, 1878 to date.

United States. Department of Labor. Bureau of Labor Statistics. *BLS Handbook of Methods*. Bureau of Labor Statistics Bulletin 2285. Washington, D.C.: Government Printing Office, 1988.

——. *Monthly Labor Review* (monthly since 1915).

——. *The Consumer Price Index: Concepts and Content over the Years*. Bureau of Labor Statistics Report 517, rev. ed. Washington, D.C.: Government Printing Office, 1978.

United States. Department of State. *Report of the Secretary of State*, [John Quincy Adams] *upon Weights and Measures*. 16th Congress, 2d. Session. Senate Documents, Vol. 4, Doc. 119. [Serial Set 45.] House Documents, Vol. 8, Doc. 109. [Serial Set 55.] Washington, D.C.: Gales and Seaton, 1821.

United States. Laws and Statutes, etc. *The Statutes at Large of the United States of America*. Ed. Richard Peters, George Minot, and George P. Sanger. 17 vols. Boston: Little, Brown and Company, 1845–73. Title varies.

United States. President. *Economic Report of the President*. Washington, D.C.: Government Printing Office, 1947 to date.

Value, Capital, and Growth: Papers in Honour of Sir John Hicks. Ed. J[ames] N. Wolfe. Edinburgh: Edinburgh University Press, 1967.

Varieties of Monetary Reforms: Lessons and Experiences on the Road to Monetary Union. Ed. Pierre L. Siklos. Boston: Kluwer Academic Publishers, [1994].

Vigneti, P. V. N. *Changes faits sur le cours des papiers-monnoies, depuis leur origine, 31 août 1789, jusqu'au 30 ventôse de l'an IV . . . auquel on a joint un tableau progressif de dépréciation vraie. . . .* Paris: Gueffier and the Author, 1797.

Vries, Jan de. 'Between Purchasing Power and the World of Goods: Understanding the Household Economy in Early Modern Europe.' In *Consumption and the World of Goods*, ed. John Brewer and Roy Potter, 85–132. London and New York: Routledge, 1993.

Warner, Sam Bass, Jr. *Writing Local History: The Use of Social Statistics*. Technical Leaflet 7. Rev. ed. Nashville, Tenn.: American Association for State and Local History, 1970.

Warren, G[eorge] F., F[rank] A. Pearson, and Herman M. Stoker. *Wholesale Prices for 213 Years, 1720 to 1932*. Cornell University Agricultural Experiment Station Memoir 412. Ithaca, N.Y.: Cornell University, 1932.

Washington, George. *The Writings of George Washington*. Ed. John C. Fitzpatrick. 39 vols. Washington, D.C.: United States Government Printing Office, [1931–1944].

Watson, Mark W. 'Business-Cycle Durations and Postwar Stabilization of the U.S. Economy.' *American Economic Review*, 84 (March 1994): 24–46.

Webster, Pelatiah. *Political Essays on the Nature and Operation of Money, Public Finances, and Other Subjects: Published during the American War, and Continued to the Present Year, 1791*. Philadelphia: Joseph Crukshank, 1791.

Wesley Clair Mitchell: The Economic Scientist. Ed. Arthur F. Burns. New York: National Bureau of Economic Research, 1952.

Wetzel, William A. *Benjamin Franklin as an Economist*. Johns Hopkins University Studies in Historical and Political Science, 13th Ser., No. 9. Baltimore: The Johns Hopkins University Press, 1895.

White, Eugene N. 'Measuring the French Revolution's Inflation: The Tableaux de depreciation.' *Histoire & Mesure*, 6 (Nos. 3/4, 1991): 245–74.

Woodward, Donald [M.] 'Wage Rates and Living Standards in Pre-Industrial England.' *Past & Present: A Journal of Historical Studies*, 91 (May 1981): 28–46.

Wright, J[ohn]. *The American Negotiator: or the Various Currencies of the British Colonies in America; As Well the Islands, as the Continent . . . Reduced into English Money . . .* 3d ed. London: The Author, 1767.

Wrigley, E[dward] A., and R. S. Schofield. *The Population History of England, 1641–1871: A Reconstruction*. Cambridge: Harvard University Press, 1981.

Wynne, Mark A., and Fiona D. Sigalla. 'The Consumer Price Index.' *Economic Review—Federal Reserve Bank of Dallas*, [74] (Second Quarter, 1994): 1–22.

Zarnowitz, Victor, and Geoffrey H. Moore. 'Major Changes in Cyclical Behavior.' In *The American Business Cycle: Continuity and Change*, ed. Robert J. Gordon. National Bureau of Economic Research, Studies in Business Cycles, Vol. 25: 519–82. Chicago: University of Chicago Press, 1986.

Index

Business Cycle Reconsidered: New Estimates of Gross National Product, 1869–1908,' 107n

Rostow, W[alt] W., *The World Economy: History & Prospect*; and Michael Kennedy, 'A Simple Model of the Kondratieff Cycle,' 28n

Rothenberg, Winifred B[arr], 'The Emergence of a Capital Market in Rural Massachusetts, 1730–1838,' 73n; *From Market-Places to a Market Economy: The Transformation of Rural Massachusetts, 1750–1850*, 48n; 'A Price Index for Rural Massachusetts, 1750–1855,' 41n, 43n, 48n; Review of *How Much Is That in Real Money? A Historical Price Index for Use as a Deflator of Money Values in the Economy of the United States*, 11n

Ruist, Erik, Ethel D. Hoover, and Philip J. McCarthy, 'Index Numbers,' 17n

S

Samuelson, Paul A., and William D. Nordhaus, *Economics*, 28n

Scale of Depreciation, Agreeable to An Act of the (Now) Commonwealth of Massachusetts, Passed September 29, 1780, 19n

Schilke, Oscar G., and Raphael E. Solomon, *America's Foreign Coins*, 37n, 62n, 86n

Schneider, Jürgen, et al., *Währungen der Welt*, 83n

Schumpeter, Joseph A., *History of Economic Analysis*, 24

Schumpeter, [Romaine] Elizabeth Boody, 'English Prices and Public Finance, 1660–1822,' 90n, 106n; Schumpeter-Gilboy, 95–99

Scott, William Robert, *The Constitution and Finance of English, Scottish, and Irish Joint-Stock Companies to 1720*, 92n

Second Hundred Years' War, 35n

Silver, 32n, 37n, 44, 62, 83n, 84; *see also* Dollar; Metals, precious

Smith, Adam, *An Inquiry into the Nature and Causes of the Wealth of Nations*, 14

Smith, Billy G., '"The Best Poor Man's Country": Living Standards of the "Lower Sort" in Late Eighteenth-Century Philadelphia,' 41n; *The 'Lower Sort': Philadelphia's Laboring People, 1750–1800*, 41n

Smith, S[imon] D., 'The Market for Manufactures in the Thirteen Continental Colonies, 1698–1776,' 23n, 35n

Solomon, Raphael E., 'Foreign Specie Coins in the American Colonies,' 62n

An Accurate Table, Ascertaining the Progressive Depreciation of the Paper-Currency, in the Province of South-Carolina, 74n

South Carolina, 34, 66–70, 73n, 75, 78–79, 85, 86; *The Statutes at Large of South Carolina*, 85n; *see also* Charleston

Spain, 35, 80, 81

Stabilization of the Domestic and International Economy, 28n

Stagflation, 29

The Statistical History of the United States from the Colonial Times to the Present, 42n

Steuart, Charles, Papers of, 81

Studies on Money in Early America, 62

Sumner, W[illiam] G., 'The Spanish Dollar and the Colonial Shilling,' 81n

T

A Table Shewing the Value of Old Tenor Bills, in Lawful Money, 19n

Tables: discussion of the use of, 35, 35n, 70n; compilation of, 10, 33, 44, 63, 91n, 92, 107; sources for data in, 34, 46n, 60n, 70n, 79n, 90, 91

Taylor, George Rogers, 42; 'Wholesale Commodity Prices at Charleston, South Carolina, [1732–1861],' 43n

Taylor/Hoover index, 42, 42n, 43, 47, 50–58

Temin, Peter, 'Labour Scarcity and Capital Markets in America,' 92

Thomas, Lloyd B., Jr., 'Survey Measures of Expected U.S. Inflation,' 60n

Tobin, James, 'Fisher, Irving,' 24n

Torelli, Sue, 20n

A Treatise of Taxes & Contributions: Shewing the Nature and Measures of Crown-Lands, 14

Turvey, Ralph, *Consumer Price Indexes: An ILO Manual*, 17n

U

Ulmer, Melville J., *The Economic Theory of Cost of Living Index Numbers*, 27n

United States: Congress, *American State*